ACA 1281

The Sun Still Shone

Professors Talk about Retirement

UNIVERSITY OF IOWA PRESS ψ Iowa City

The Sun Still Shone

Lorraine T. Dorfman

University of Iowa Press,

Iowa City 52242

Copyright © 1997 by the University of Iowa Press

All rights reserved

Printed in the United States of America

Design by Richard Hendel

http://www.uiowa.edu/~uipress

Library of Congress Cataloging-in-Publication Data

Dorfman, Lorraine T.

    The sun still shone: professors talk about retirement / by
  Lorraine T. Dorfman.

        p.   cm.

    Includes bibliographical references (p.   ) and index.

    ISBN 0-87745-601-1

    1. College teachers—United States—Retirement.   2. College
  teachers—Great Britain—Retirement.   3. College teachers—
  United States—Interviews.   4. College teachers—Great Britain—
  Interviews.   I. Title.

  LB2334.D67   1997

  331.25′2—dc21   97-16580

  02   01   00   99   98   97   C   5   4   3   2   1

For Don

Contents

Acknowledgments

Many people, institutions, and agencies helped make this book a reality. Support for my work over the years came from a number of sources, including the Multidisciplinary Gerontology Center of Iowa, a University House/Andrew W. Mellon Foundation Grant, a Midwest Universities Consortium for International Activities travel grant, a University of Iowa Old Gold Fellowship, and two semester developmental assignments from the University of Iowa. The first semester assignment was to conduct the interviews in the United Kingdom; the more recent semester assignment, in 1996, provided me with a block of time to write the book. Without that period free from other academic responsibilities, the project could not have come to fruition. I would also like to acknowledge the support services provided by the Obermann Center for Advanced Studies at the University of Iowa, where I was housed when I wrote the book. The Center offered me a quiet and congenial place to work without interruption. Particular thanks go to its director, Jay Semel, who knows how to deal well with a bunch of faculty scholars, and to its marvelous and always helpful secretary, Lorna Olson. I also thank the administrations of the Universities of Iowa, Liverpool, and Manchester, Drake University, and Augustana, Coe, and Cornell Colleges for their cooperation.

My collaborators from the liberal arts colleges and comprehensive university, Jean Tompkins of Cornell College, William Ward of Augustana College, and Karen Conner of Drake University, were a pleasure to work with and provided many helpful insights about those institutions. Additionally, a number of graduate research assistants helped in interviewing, computing, and transcribing over the years. Thanks go to Elizabeth Hill, Cynthia Kirk, Mildred Moffett, Mary Willie, Carol Mertens, Sang-In Nam, Jennifer Schmidt, and Lisa Braun for all their hard work. Holly Carver of the University of Iowa

Press provided much encouragement and assistance; I am grateful that she was at the same time both caring and careful of this book and its author. My faithful and efficient secretary in the School of Social Work, Madelyn Bowersox, helped put the final product together, and, as always, I am in her debt for her work and her forbearance.

My greatest thanks, however, go to my husband, Donald D. Dorfman, for his love and his unfailing support of my professional endeavors for nearly four decades. In our shared life together and from his example, I learned early on what a professor could be.

The Sun Still Shone

Introduction

"It's a closing of one phase and a beginning of another."

a sixty-five-year-old male professor of speech pathology

For many professors, retirement offers the opportunity to focus on what they liked best during their preretirement careers. Professors often view their life's work as a calling that will continue throughout their adult years. Unlike most occupational groups, for whom retirement means the cessation of the former work role, professors often have the opportunity to continue some aspects of their work during the retirement years. This is institutionalized in many colleges and universities in the rank of emeritus professor, which, although flexible and not universal, usually accords the holder certain rights and privileges which allow for a degree of role continuity in retirement. It is therefore not surprising that many professors continue some aspects of their work role during the retirement years, albeit at a generally reduced pace. Some continue their research or other creative work, while others find opportunities for part-time teaching or consulting. Other professors, however, choose to spend the bulk of their time in nonprofessional leisure or service pursuits. To date, few works exist that allow professors to talk at length about these lifestyle choices or about how they evaluate the retirement experience. The voices of professors who are already retired can offer valuable insights for future retirees and, at the same time, can provide a rich understanding of their lives as professionals.

Large numbers of professors were hired during the decade of the 1960s due to the burgeoning enrollments that characterized higher education during those years. The children of the baby boom that swept this country shortly after World War II were entering colleges and universities in record numbers and needed to be accommodated. Many of the professors who were hired during that period are now in their fifties and sixties. Large numbers of them are expected to retire in the next ten years. According to the National Center for Education Statistics (*Digest of Educational Statistics*), there are presently nearly nine hundred thousand professors teaching in institutions of higher education in the United States, up from less than seven hundred thousand twenty years ago. Many of those professors would like to know what to expect as they grow older. Likewise, many professors who are already retired would like to know of the experiences of others who, like themselves, are already retired. Higher education planners and administrators also need to know as much as possible about older professors in order to facilitate development of older faculty and to aid in institutional planning on retirement. This information is particularly important in light of the elimination of mandatory retirement in higher education in 1994. It would be useful for institutional planners to know, for instance, how retired academics evaluate the institutional assistance that was given to them in preparing for retirement, how well various retirement options worked out, and how professors see themselves as being effectively utilized as they grow older.

Many questions remain to be explored regarding the retirement experience of professors. Why do some professors continue their work after retirement while others completely abandon it? How is retirement different for professors from different disciplines — for instance, from the sciences and the humanities? For professors who taught in colleges and those who taught in universities? For men and women? What happens to professors who live to reach their eighties and nineties? Is the experience of American professors unique, or are there parallels in other countries?

Nearly all that has been written about the lives of professors in retirement has been quantitative in nature and has been presented as grouped information (see appendix A for major sources). In this book, in contrast, I use qualitative case materials to let professors describe the retirement experience in their own voices. I thus aim to convey the variety, quality, and richness of the individual retirement experience. Each person confronts life's transitions and deals with a changing environment in his or her own way. By exploring a range of reactions to one of the major transitions of later life — retirement — we may be able to achieve a fuller understanding of how people deal with their own aging. From this range of experiences, common themes and patterns arise. These themes and patterns, along with the individual experiences of the retired professors, are explored throughout this book.

Background

In 1978 I began a series of interview studies of retired professors that continued for more than ten years. Relatively little research on retired professors had been conducted prior to that time. The goal of these studies was to explore the professional and nonprofessional activities of professors in retirement and their reactions to the retirement experience. The initial study, conducted between 1978 and 1980, included all retired professors from a public research university (the University of Iowa). A comparative study of retired professors from three liberal arts colleges (Augustana, Coe, and Cornell Colleges) and a comprehensive university (Drake University) in Iowa and Illinois was conducted in 1980–1981 in order to explore similarities and differences in the retirement experience of professors from different kinds of institutions. This was followed in 1983–1984 by a study of retired professors from two "old civic" universities in the United Kingdom (the Universities of Liverpool and Manchester). Findings from that study were compared to those for professors from the public research university in the United States. To my knowledge, this comparative study is the only existing cross-national study of retired academics. Since old civic universities in the United Kingdom are most similar in history, purpose, and student body composition to American state universities, they provide a suitable comparison to the American public research university. By studying retired academics from different kinds of institutions and from another nation, my colleagues and I were able to explore the retirement experience of academics in various social contexts. A final set of interviews was conducted over an eleven-year period (1979 to 1989) with professors from the public research university in order to better understand the period of transition to retirement. Professors were interviewed within six months prior to their retirement and again one year after their retirement, thus giving them the opportunity to discuss retirement both before and after the event. Since only about a dozen faculty retired from the university each year, it took about a decade to gather material from a significant number of professors.

During the late 1970s and early 1980s, phased retirement and special incentive early retirement plans were available only at the American comprehensive university and at some of the liberal arts colleges. A small number of professors chose those plans and are included in the case materials presented here. Phased and special incentive early retirement plans became available at the American research university a number of years after the transition to retirement study was already under way; therefore, professors who chose those plans are not represented here. Additionally, community college retirees are not included, because it was decided to restrict the study to retirees from four-year institutions. The case materials in this book are based on interviews with retired academics from colleges and universities in the Midwest in the United States and the Northwest in England; they may therefore not be representative of retired academics from other regions of the two countries. The case materials do not claim to represent all academic retirees. The interview materials can, however, be considered reasonably representative of retired professors from several major kinds of institutions in the United States and the United Kingdom.

In all, 113 professors from the public research university, 54 professors from the liberal arts colleges, 36 professors from the comprehensive university, 124 professors from the British universities, and 104 professors in the longitudinal transition to retirement study agreed to participate. Fewer British retirees (62 percent) agreed to participate than did American retirees, whose participation ranged from 82 percent for the comprehensive university to 87 percent for the liberal arts colleges. There were several reasons for this difference in willingness to participate. One major reason was the method of recruitment. British universities permitted potential respondents to be approached only indirectly through a university mailing; respondents were asked in this mailing to contact the investigator if they were willing to be interviewed. American respondents, in contrast, were identified by name by their institutions and could be contacted directly. Second, there appeared to be a greater emphasis on privacy in the United Kingdom than in the United States. This was evidenced by the written refusals to participate, all saying that one's private life was not an appropriate topic for study. Finally, more of the British academics may have been too ill to be interviewed; however, it was not possible to determine their numbers, as it was in the United States.

The interview schedule contained both tape-recorded open-ended questions and a written questionnaire. The tape-recorded questions were designed to provide a qualitative assessment of reactions to the retirement experience. The questionnaire segment of the interview schedule, consisting mainly of forced-choice and scale items, was designed to provide a more quantitative assessment of attitudinal and behavioral responses (see appendix A for published articles based on the questionnaire). Personal interviews were conducted by me, by several colleagues at the liberal arts colleges and the comprehensive university, and in the case of the transition to retirement study, by trained graduate students at the University of Iowa. Not all respondents were willing to answer the open-ended questions or consent to be tape-recorded. In addition, a small number of tapes were unintelligible. As a result, the case materials in this book are based on a total of 409 tape recordings with 327 individuals: 98 from the research university, 46 from the liberal arts colleges, 23 from the comprehensive university, 64 from the British universities, and 96 from the longitudinal transition to retirement study. Professors who left their pre-retirement communities after retiring were generally interviewed by telephone, and the responses were tape-recorded. A small number of handwritten responses from the British retirees who left their pre-retirement communities after retiring are also included in the case materials. The interview schedule was mailed to British respondents who had left their preretirement communities because they were scattered all over the United Kingdom and abroad. Poor internal telephone connections in the United Kingdom at the time the materials were collected precluded telephone interviews, which were possible for most of the retirees who had left their preretirement communities in the United States.

Content analysis categories representing the major themes that emerged from the tapes were constructed on the basis of the tape-recorded open-ended interview materials. Individual responses were coded into appropriate content analysis categories by two independent coders who listened to the tapes. Excerpts from the tapes were transcribed by me and by a trained graduate student to illustrate each content analysis category. Those edited excerpts, conveying the quality and range of responses to retirement, are the basis for this book. Obviously, not all comments from the more than four hundred interview tapes could be included. The ones that were selected illustrate important points that the retired academics made about the retirement experience. Consequently, one excerpt may illustrate a point that was made by many respondents. The more articulate responses are admittedly overrepresented. Every effort was made, however, to fairly represent all opinions and points of view that were expressed. Frequencies of responses to the various content analysis categories were tabulated and are also included; however, the emphasis in this book is on letting the retired academics describe the retirement experience in their own voices. I have tried to remain as true as possible to the interview tapes. In some cases, because respondents' voices were low or muffled or because accents were difficult to discern, some words may have been lost. The sense of the tapes, however, is always retained. Occasionally, excerpts from different parts of a single interview tape are combined when they are a response to a question asked earlier or when they represent the same thought. In order to increase readability, no ellipses are used when there are pauses or digressions on the tapes. To protect confidentiality, no respondents are identified by name. Instead, they are identified only by age, discipline, sex, and type of institution. Names are changed whenever respondents refer to their colleagues or to other persons by name. Also to preserve confidentiality, references to the academics' preretirement cities and institutions are deleted.

It is frequently assumed that older people are rather homogeneous, with age being their defining characteristic. The characteristics of the academic retirees represented here do not substantiate this myth. The median age of the retired academics from both the United States and the United Kingdom was seventy-three years, with a range of from sixty-six to one hundred years in the United States and sixty-two to ninety-two years in the United Kingdom. The academics had been retired for one to thirty-two years. Professors in the longitudinal transition to retirement study were considerably younger than those in the other studies, because they were all interviewed around the time of retirement. The median age of those professors was sixty-eight years at the preretirement interview, with an age range of fifty-two to seventy-one years. With respect to age at retirement, the American academics were more likely to retire at the age that was mandatory for their institutions than were the British academics. The mandatory age ranged from sixty-five at the American liberal arts colleges to seventy at the comprehensive university. British academics typically retired at age sixty-five, although the mandatory retirement age for their institutions was sixty-seven.

The vast majority (more than 80 percent) of retirees from all institutions except the American liberal arts colleges were men. One-third of the retirees from the liberal arts colleges were women. About 70 percent of the respondents in both the United States and the United Kingdom were married at the time of the interview; however, there were marked gender differences in marital status. Men were far more likely to be married (86 percent) than were women (22 percent). Furthermore, most of the unmarried women had never been married (65 percent), whereas only a small percentage of men had never been married (16 percent). With respect to other marital statuses, there were more widowed retirees in the United Kingdom than in the United States (20 percent compared to 12 percent), but fewer never-married people (8 percent compared to between 13 and 17 percent for the various American institutions). The percentage of separated or divorced retirees was low in both countries, ranging from

2 percent to 4 percent at particular institutions. Since the respondents in the transition to retirement study were all within one year of retirement and were therefore younger than the other respondents, they were more likely to be still married than were the other retirees (84 percent).

Although there were a number of respondents who were in poor health, the overall health of the retired academics was quite good, at least in terms of their self-evaluations. Academics were asked to rate their own health compared to other people their own age on a scale of 0 to 100, with 0 equal to "extremely poor," 50 equal to "average," and 100 equal to "extremely good." The average ratings on the 100 point scale were quite high, ranging from 78 to 80 for academics from the various types of American institutions. The average health rating for the British academics was similar, at 76.

At the time of the interview, there was a very large income spread among the retirees, ranging from about $1,000 to over $100,000. The median annual income was $19,500 for American research university retirees, $17,000 for comprehensive university retirees, and $12,000 for liberal arts college retirees. Thus, liberal arts college retirees had substantially lower incomes than did their university counterparts. Median annual income for the British academics (in dollars) was slightly more than two-thirds that of academics from the comparison American research university. Retirees in the research university transition to retirement study had a higher annual median income than did other retirees ($32,000), reflecting their more recent retirement. With respect to gender, female retirees across institutions had substantially lower incomes than did their male counterparts. The median annual income of all male academics who were interviewed was $22,500, nearly double that of female academics ($12,750). The majority of retirees, both female and male, said that their standard of living was approximately the same as before retirement.

A final methodological note on language: in the United Kingdom, "academic staff" is the term used to describe persons holding academic rank. The term "professor" is used to designate only those few individuals holding professorships. In contrast, in the United States, all individuals holding academic rank at the assistant professor level or above are designated "professor." I shall use the terms "retired professor" and "retired academic" synonymously throughout the book. Additionally, in the United Kingdom, the term "faculty" is often used to denote a department or larger academic unit (e.g., the faculty of sociology, the faculty of education), whereas the terms "department" and "school" are used in the United States.

Overview of the Book

There is a relatively small literature on retired professors, most of which focuses on activity patterns in retirement and adjustment to retirement. In a thoughtful paper delivered at the March 1994 annual meeting of the Midwest Sociological Society ("Recent Trends in Faculty Retirement Research"), William C. Lane notes a turning away in recent years from fundamental issues of social processes and individual adjustment of retired professors to a focus on the effects of legislative changes on institutions of higher education. Specifically, this latter body of research involves the impact of first extending and then uncapping, or removing, the mandatory retirement age and institutional responses to this uncapping such as phased retirement and early retirement incentive plans. Because the numbers of older and retired faculty are currently increasing dramatically, Lane urges a return to the most basic and fundamental questions in academic retirement such as life patterns and individual adjustment, away from the institutional focus of the past decade. In support of his view, the National Research Council estimates that the largest age group of current faculty will be entering their sixties in the next decade and thus approaching retirement age (*Ending Mandatory Retirement for Tenured Faculty*).

This book addresses some of the basic issues in retirement adaptation. It is thus concerned with the process of retirement. Chapter 2 examines getting ready for retirement, including professors' feelings about their approaching retirement and perceived changes in behavior of their colleagues and students, as well as specific plans for and timing of retirement and reactions to institutional retirement plans. Chapter 3 addresses the decision of where to live after retirement and explores reasons for staying in or leaving the preretirement community. Chapter 4 describes professors' evaluation of the retirement experience, both positive and negative, and offers their suggestions for others who are soon to retire. Activity patterns in retirement are described in chapters 5 and 6. Chapter 5 examines the various types and levels of continued professional activity in retirement, including research or other creative work, teaching, consulting, and clinical work or practice. The institutional opportunity structure or climate for continued professional work and job opportunities is also explored. Chapter 6 examines the nonprofessional leisure and service activities of retired professors. Interinstitutional and cross-national comparisons are made throughout. A final summary chapter examines common themes and patterns in the lives of retired professors, with implications for faculty development and the utilization of older faculty. Some questions for the future are also raised in the concluding chapter, including possible differences between successive age cohorts of retired professors, the effects of the end of mandatory retirement on individual retirement decisions, and variations in the retirement experiences of non-Western and non-English-speaking professors.

It is through the eyes and voices of retired professors that we can best understand the richness and variety of their experience of later life. These are people who have spent their lives in intellectually challenging pursuits; highly verbal, they tell us not only about the experience of their old age, but a great deal about the full span of their lives. As a new Ph.D. embarking in 1978 in my own midlife on an academic career, I wondered, "What happens to academics as they grow old? Does it all end when they retire?" In these pages, I try to tell their story. We begin now by turning to how the academics prepared for retirement.

Getting Ready

"Planning for the future is important and also

difficult in a rapidly changing world."

a seventy-six-year-old male professor

of religion and philosophy

Although there is no longer a mandatory retirement age in higher education, the vast majority of academics still choose to retire somewhere between the ages of sixty-five and seventy. This is at least several years later than the typical retirement age for the general population. Academics retire for pretty much the same reasons as do other groups: the desire to have more flexibility in how one's time is spent, loss of involvement with work, lack of fit in the current workplace, and declining energy and health.

Getting ready for retirement is a process that may occur over a considerable period. It includes not only making specific plans for retirement such as financial planning, where to live, and how to spend one's time, but also dealing with one's feelings about the retirement stage of life, about one's career, and about the attitudes of other people. We know that people who plan for retirement and give prior thought to retirement tend to adjust better to retirement than do people who do not prepare for retirement. Thus, it appears advantageous to engage in what sociologists call anticipatory socialization, or practice, for future roles.

Feelings about Approaching Retirement

In order to tap attitudes about their approaching retirement, professors in the transition to retirement study at the American research university were asked: "In general, how do you feel about your approaching retirement?" Their responses, not unexpectedly, expressed a wide variety of reactions to their upcoming retirements. Nearly three-fourths of the professors said they were looking forward to retirement. A sixty-five-year-old professor of speech pathology communicated his positive view:

> In a sense it's a closing of one phase and a beginning of another in our lives — my own and my wife's. I don't plan to be deeply involved in the academic affairs that I have been involved in throughout my career at the university. In recent years, I have become more involved in environmental affairs. What I'm really looking forward to is having more time to be an active environmentalist. I think I have a few good years left. I'm also going to build a house.

Many professors looked forward to retirement as a time when they could perhaps live a more balanced life of leisure and professional activities. This kind of life was planned by a male engineer, aged sixty-eight, from the research university:

> I feel very good about it, because I've considered what I shall need to do to be satisfied when I'm no longer challenged and satisfied with the work that I've spent a lifetime doing and have enjoyed. So I've found the things I shall do instead. I hesitate to even call them substitutes because that always suggests that it's second best, but I realize the intellectual challenge that my work has given me and I realize that I must continue that. I don't think anyone who's lived my kind of life could think of going fishing every day as a new way of life. I like to fish and intend to fish, and I'll probably spend a lot more time fishing and gardening and doing many other things. I have a lot of hobbies, none of which I do very well, but I will have

a good time with all of those, and I'll spend more time than I've been able to in my lab. I think one must continue to spend time in what one has spent a lifetime doing.

A sixty-eight-year-old male professor of biochemistry said simply, "I'm very optimistic. I think that's part of my nature," whereas a sixty-two-year-old female health educator admitted that "it's going to be a very wrenching experience to leave the university and this community, but I want to do other things."

On the other hand, some people were very negative about their approaching retirement. Retirement may be difficult particularly for scientists who want to continue their work and need substantial support for that work. A seventy-year-old male chemist, who was retiring at the mandatory age, put it this way:

I feel terrible. I think it varies with people. In other words, in my case I've always been active next door in the laboratory. Just to cut that thing off. I've got enough things going that another year or so of tapering off would be great. But it's going to be hard to get it. For some other people that don't work in the lab, I suppose it doesn't make any difference. Suggesting dropping everything immediately is ridiculous. If I want to continue it I need to find a place.

Faculty from other disciplines, however, also expressed negative attitudes about retiring, particularly if they were retiring at the mandatory age. A seventy-year-old member of the Spanish and Portuguese department spoke of his desire to stay on: "I'm not ready to retire. I have plenty of experience and enthusiasm. I think I can work for ten or fifteen more years."

There were also those who were ambivalent about their approaching retirement and expressed quite mixed feelings. The response from a male professor of photography, aged seventy, is typical: "I have a dual response to it. One where I can't believe it's happening and don't want to do it. I guess I've gotten a lot of feedback from the students and I like teaching very much. It took a lot of energy that I didn't have the same amount of."

Some of the most moving comments were from people who had

not yet quite come to grips with the reality of retirement. Essentially, they denied the reality of retirement and felt that it was not really happening to them. Here is the strategy adopted by a male professor of physiology and biophysics, aged seventy: "I don't feel that I'm retiring. I'm willing to say to friends that really I'm not retiring. So I've given myself the title of senior professor without pay."

Perceived Changes in Behavior of Colleagues and Students

Some professors in the transition to retirement study noticed positive changes in their colleagues and students as retirement approached. Some even felt that their colleagues and students were more positive and supportive than they had been previously. This positive reaction was expressed by a male musician, aged sixty-eight:

> If I've noticed any changes, they've been more appreciative and expressed their feelings more than they do at other times. In fact, I've been flattered by the many expressions of appreciation for my work both by students, townspeople, and acquaintances. I gave my final concert the other night and they gave me a wonderful reception. We had a couple of hundred people in after the concert, and they gave me a lovely original print. And I'm having concerts dedicated to me by bands and, you know, the kind of thing that's really awfully nice and unexpected. In my case, people in the last year have made a special effort to be nicer than ever.

A professor of religion, aged sixty-five, likewise commented on how gratified he was with reactions from his colleagues:

> Very congenial. The School of Religion, for example, put on a nice big dinner at the Holiday Inn for me. The pastoral services here put on a party last Saturday night at one of their houses. It was definitely because of my retirement, so it was kind of commemorating it and celebrating it, and I found positive support. In other words, I found my thinking about my retirement and the thinking of my colleagues is pretty compatible. I haven't had a lot of people saying, "Oh, we can't do without you; you've got to stay on; how can you possibly leave us?" On the other hand, I haven't had

people saying, "It's about time." We've all been on the same wavelength about it.

Yet, when behavioral changes of colleagues or students were reported, they most frequently tended to be negative. Those perceived changes in colleagues and students seemed to communicate to the retiring professor that he or she was no longer needed, was no longer valued, was being put out to pasture. Two professors from disciplines as diverse as business administration and chemistry illustrated these feelings. The former man was retiring at the mandatory age of seventy, whereas the latter man was retiring a few years earlier, at age sixty-seven:

> Yes, I've noticed changes in colleagues. Only some of them, however, it's not a general thing. On occasion you do see them. The change is particularly that they discount you, they've written you off. That's what that previous fear that I mentioned comes out of. You lose identity. They figure there's nothing they can get out of you anymore.

> I notice changes in behavior mainly in the last few weeks. People say, gee, I thought you were already gone. I was home with the flu and got tied up for several weeks and since I've been on leave I don't come over to the building much. And the reaction of the students when the information got around was that's a rumor, but it turned out to be true this time. Rumors have gone around earlier that I was going to retire, a number of years ago. And the rumor went around this time, but it was true. A number of students were upset because they wanted to take a class I was going to teach. That's the main kind of reaction from students. The reaction from graduate students had been going on for a number of years because I had been turning down students as possible advisees for thesis work for quite a number of years because it wouldn't be fair. I haven't had a graduate student now on a long program for about three years.

A professor of rhetoric, aged sixty-five, added concerns about being treated differently due to the inevitable, and observable, physical changes that accompany aging. For her, these changes were intertwined with retirement:

> There's a sense of putting you on the shelf. You aren't consulted as often. There's obviously terminitis. There's another change that isn't necessarily related to retirement but it seems to go along with aging. In the last five to eight years, my appearance has changed remarkably and as you shift from middle age you can see people shutting you out, the invisible man, the invisible woman.

Planning for Retirement

A large majority of retired professors from all of the American colleges and universities said they had thought seriously about retirement and made financial plans. A majority had also checked on what retirement benefits were available from their college or university and had discussed retirement with their friends or colleagues. Interestingly, a larger percentage of comprehensive university professors had engaged in financial planning for retirement and had also checked on retirement benefits and inquired about facilities for continued work after retirement than had professors from the research university and the liberal arts colleges, probably reflecting the existence of a preretirement planning center at the comprehensive university during the 1970s. This suggests that when retirement planning assistance exists professors will use it.

Differences in the preretirement planning experience of British and American academics were also found. A significantly larger percentage of American academics had made financial plans for retirement and had inquired about university and departmental facilities available for retirees than had British academics. The difference in financial planning for retirement between American and British academics may reflect the relatively greater financial benefits of the welfare state in the United Kingdom compared to the United States.

A number of retirees spoke of the considerable amount of thought that had gone into their retirement planning process. An eighty-year-old liberal arts college geologist recalled the methodical planning that he had done prior to his retirement twelve years earlier:

I certainly did a lot of thinking about it. I reviewed my insurance program and made sure that our wills were up to date. We talked things over with our attorney. It was never a part of our thinking, at least in the last twenty or thirty years, to go elsewhere. We had a home that we thought we would enjoy much more than anything we could pick up anywhere else. Neither Florida nor California offered any attraction for us so great that we contemplated selling and moving. We have kept everything in reasonably good condition through the years. We did things that were dictated by the changing times, like getting good insulation. I attended no seminars or books other than what TIAA [Teachers Insurance and Annuity Association] put out.

A liberal arts college professor, aged eighty-four, from the department of education spoke of the importance of being psychologically prepared for retirement. The determination of this woman is clear in her voice: "Well, I just made a survey of conditions and appreciated that I was completely out of that work, and I would make the best of what's left. That was it. It was a psychological preparation, that is true, but I knew some were kind of sour about it, but I never felt that way."

Just as with other important transitions in life, preparing for retirement involves a great deal of learning from informal sources. Family, friends, and colleagues, as well as reading about retirement, are important sources of information and can help reduce the uncertainties and ambiguities of retirement. A sixty-seven-year-old English professor, also from one of the liberal arts colleges, described those influences on her planning:

Well, we read some material on income tax and somebody gave us a book on things to think about before retirement that we both read with considerable interest. It didn't all apply to us, but some of it did. It was really aimed at business people, primarily. It was helpful. I think we tended to listen to the experiences of retired friends. We noted that some of our retired friends got ulcers the first year of their retirement. We paid more attention to how people were adjusting to retirement.

Similarly, a sixty-seven-year-old comprehensive university professor of education said: "Well, I did a lot of reading about it. And getting the various publications and talking with friends and colleagues." In contrast, his colleague, a seventy-two-year-old female mathematician, noted that retirement is basically a personal and family decision: "I listened to them, but actually it was a decision between my husband and myself."

Financial planning for retirement is, of course, fundamental to the planning process. Many professors spoke of the steps they had taken to try to ensure that their financial situation would be adequate in retirement. The following steps were outlined by a seventy-four-year-old male astronomer from the comprehensive university:

> Of course I watched my finances pretty closely. I made every effort to increase my savings for the last eight or ten years, which is about the length of time I had the ability to do any significant saving. That was probably the number one thing, watch the money and plan for how you're going to handle the retirement pension, find out what your Social Security is going to be, and look at your life insurance.

Concerns about meeting costs of basic needs, especially health care, were more common among the older retirees. This seventy-six-year-old male liberal arts college professor of religion and philosophy was acutely aware of the increasing cost of health care as people grow older and more frail:

> Planning for the future is important and also difficult in a rapidly changing world. One who has to worry about meeting basic needs for food, clothing, shelter, and medical care finds it hard to be truly happy. I believe that all colleges have TIAA and CREF [College Retirement Equities Fund] plans for retirement income and also tax-sheltered annuity plans. These help but are not enough. Social Security has been a life-saver. Blue Cross, Blue Shield, and other medical plans need to be explored. Many colleges have plans for major medical expenses. Health care becomes increasingly expensive with advancing years — eyes, ears, teeth, and other parts of the body require more care and more expense. Needs for hospitals, surgeons, nursing homes, and nursing care have to be considered. Again, Medicare is of great assistance but doesn't cover all expenses. It is wise and economical to do everything one can to

prevent disease and keep healthy, but as age advances one cannot expect to do this forever.

Planning for use of large amounts of newly found free time is of major importance in preparing for retirement, because there are now twenty-four hours a day seven days a week to fill. Being able to use this time in a meaningful, productive, and rewarding way is of central concern for most retirees. What this male liberal arts college professor of English, aged seventy-two, did was plan ahead for a new activity in retirement:

My preparations for retirement were really preparations for what I was going to do in retirement. That was to set up this photographic shop. Therefore I had to make certain financial arrangements. I had to find a place on Main Street that I could rent. And make certain decisions as to when to open. I had to remodel the inside of this place I have rented so that I could have a darkroom and a studio and a front part; divide the big room into three parts. This is the sort of practical arrangements that I had to do because I wanted to go right into it right after I retired. I was getting this ready before I actually retired in the spring, in my spare time.

For some retirees, retirement offers the opportunity to get back to a pleasurable activity that may have been put aside because of time constraints in their professional lives. A comprehensive university professor of secretarial science, now aged eighty-one, talked about her plan to resume a hobby she had enjoyed long before:

My weaving is one of the things I had done years ago. I had taken up this weaving as a hobby. I had to give it up when I had to study for my doctor's degree, and with the activity in all my professional things, I didn't have time for it. But about three years before retirement came, I knew that I was going to want to do something. I had felt when I was younger, in my thirties, that I enjoyed the weaving and it was something I would go back to. So I decided about five years before I retired that I would try it out one summer and see if I still liked it as well. I rented a loom from the art center and tried it out that summer and found out that I still did love it. I knew that was one of the things I was going to want to do.

Not the least among retirement planning issues is thinking about where to live. Most academics, like other retirement groups, do not choose to move to a new location after retiring, but instead grow old in place. For the minority of academics who do choose to move to a new location or at least to a different residence, careful planning is essential. A liberal arts college professor of French, aged seventy-two, talked about the advantages of purchasing a condominium to accommodate her new lifestyle:

I certainly looked forward to a different kind of lifestyle. I wanted to be near the center of town so I could walk to things I wanted to do. I like the outdoors and being by the lake is nice. I still think that location and looking ahead to whether you'll always be able to always live there — I'm thinking I can always get around to the things I want to go to where I am. I can always do that. I think a person has to not get to a place that's inaccessible because they'll be shut off from other people and be isolated. They have to be in a place where they can meet other people and people who they want to meet.

Visiting a place where one is considering relocating and arranging for the sale of one's present home were mentioned as important steps in retirement planning by a number of retirees in their seventies. Professors of English, library science, and philosophy, all male, from several different institutions described their relocation plans:

Well, certainly in visiting the area where we spend our November to April. That was our planning for the area. We visited there and bought a mobile home. So we knew we were going to go down there. In a sense, we bought a second home. We planned to sell our home here and move into an apartment here — that was a part of our planning. We had given thought previously to what our income would be. In a sense we'd prepared for that quite long in advance, I think.

We had owned our own home here and of course we did take steps to dispose of that, which we did in a rather fortunate way by finding people to pay the rent for a year and at the end of that time purchase it if they wished. So that solved that problem very easily.

We had purchased a home out here in Tacoma a number of years before, somewhat casually, thinking it might be useful. So there has been a little planning ahead.

When They Planned

The retired academics were asked at what age they began to make various plans for retirement. Planning for retirement typically began in the late fifties or early sixties, with the exception of financial planning, which tended to begin earlier. Interestingly, professors from both American universities typically began to make financial plans at about age forty-eight, whereas professors from the liberal arts colleges, who had lower incomes, typically began to make financial plans later, at about age fifty-five. The British academics started financial planning considerably later than did academics from any of the American institutions, at an average age of fifty-eight. The ten-year discrepancy in age of financial planning between American and British university retirees probably reflects the relatively greater financial benefits and security of the welfare state in the United Kingdom. On the other hand, academics from different kinds of institutions and from the two nations differed little in the age at which they began other kinds of retirement planning. These plans included thinking seriously about retirement, discussing it with others, checking on benefits from the college or university, and asking about what facilities were available from their department, college, or university after retirement. Some retirees spoke of the benefits of preparing for the future very early, as did this seventy-four-year-old astronomer from the comprehensive university:

> I decided when I was fourteen or fifteen that I would be self-sufficient. Certain things you roll into that. One, you are competent in your field. Two, you save money. Three, you watch to see what society is doing and try to get there ten years ahead of society. All your life you try to outguess your competition. These are the steps I would take. Any retirement counselors are starting way too late.

His sixty-nine-year-old colleague, a male business administration professor, agreed:

Why, sure, for twenty-five years. All kinds of planning. We anticipated leaving the state and that whole change of lifestyle involved many, many plans of many different types. I don't think I could make a list of them. But certainly, it involved everything we do, where we lived and what we're doing. I can't put a finger on a single point.

But then there were the minority who did little or no retirement planning at any age, as illustrated by a seventy-one-year-old male professor of speech from a liberal arts college:

Well, within the year, I didn't think about it very much in terms of preparation for what was pending. I hardly knew what was pending. I just figured I'd have to face that when it comes. I really didn't prepare for it very carefully and I still wouldn't know exactly how to prepare for it. I guess you just have to take it in stride and adjust to it as it comes.

And a seventy-five-year-old female professor of physical education, also from one of the liberal arts colleges, apparently gave no prior thought whatsoever to retirement: "I just turned the lock in the door and walked out."

Retirement Information and Assistance from the College or University

Many employers today provide information about retirement to their employees. This most commonly involves the financial aspects of retirement, but, increasingly, information on social and psychological aspects, health, housing, and family relations is also included. The retired academics were asked what information or assistance concerning retirement had been given to them by their respective institutions. Most of the information that was reported concerned financial benefits that would be available. Only a handful of retirees reported that they had received information about college or university privileges that would be available to them after retirement, about early retirement, or about preretirement preparation sessions. Professors in the transition to retirement study were more likely to report that they had received information about retirement from their institutions than were the respondents who had been retired for longer periods. This probably reflects both the recency of their having received that information and also the likelihood that college and university personnel or staff benefits offices were giving more attention to retirement issues in more recent years.

Reactions to the quality of the information or assistance received from the college or university ranged from extreme satisfaction and gratitude to great dissatisfaction. Among those who expressed positive reactions was this sixty-seven-year-old male political scientist from the comprehensive university, who appeared quite satisfied with the range of information he had received:

> I had, of course, discussions with my deans and other colleagues, a good deal of just sort of freewheeling kinds of things. I didn't go to what was deliberate questions, that kind of thing, but it was more or less a discussion: "What will you do when you retire?" And then we had other colleagues who were interested in retiring about the same time we were and we had a lot of discussions about "what-are-you-going-to-do kinds of things." And I think that's very useful. Oh yes, we got materials from time to time which were fed to us, oh, maybe a year before retirement. The administration sent us lists of data and information and book reading lists and all kinds of stuff. I can't recall the details of it, but generally they indicated that I would continue my membership in the library and have a special library card, you know, for retired persons so that I can go check out a book while I'm there if I want to or get it by mail or whatever. And also any of the other services such as athletics, music, and all those kinds of things; whatever provisions they had for that. Usually in most cases it was a reduced charge kind of thing.

Some retired academics were particularly satisfied with the financial information about retirement benefits provided by their institutions prior to retirement, as these comments from a male research university political scientist, aged sixty-eight, show:

> Well, we had a meeting with Robert Smith. At least my wife and I had, where he went through the procedure and how to fill out the forms for TIAA and CREF. He told us we should get on Medicare

at sixty-five and went down and got everything straightened out with Social Security. That's been very helpful.

But other retirees were unhappy with the information and treatment they received after what they saw as long and loyal service to their college or university. For some, like this sixty-three-year-old research university pediatrician, there was considerable dissatisfaction with information about financial benefits given by his university:

> With regards to finance, I do not think the university does a good job with regards to preparing people for retirement financially. True, they give us brochures and everything, but that's not enough. There are many people who don't know what SRAs [Supplemental Retirement Annuities] are. They don't know that they can tax defer part of their salary without much of a change in take-home pay. I've gotten into the retirement committee. I put a grievance into the retirement committee.

A professor of educational administration, aged sixty-seven, from the same university expressed his frustration this way:

> The biggest letdown is the way they handle retirement at this university. It might affect me psychologically except I teach work in personnel. For the university to be almost oblivious to the fact that they do have to provide information. They don't have to give all types of information like the fact that you need vacations, hobbies. That's kind of belittling.

Some retirees, however, like this sixty-seven-year-old professor of theater in the transition to retirement postretirement interview, were aware of and sympathetic to the strains that institutions face in being able to offer adequate personalized retirement information to large numbers of people: "I don't know the answer to it. I guess I feel that there are hundreds of faculty members and there isn't time for the university to take care of them all, but I wish there had been a little closer contact with someone in the administrative area before mine [retirement] came up."

The academics were also questioned about how the college or university might best assist people in the transition to retirement. Some respondents felt that the institution should not play a role in the transition of academics to retirement — that it was an individual matter. The majority, however, offered suggestions to their college or university. A professor of business administration, who was about to retire from the research university at the mandatory age of seventy, felt that the general treatment of retirement at his institution needed to be improved:

> There are some things that come at one, but it's not a comprehensive treatment. Another point I'd like to make is that it comes at one darn fast. I've had the impression that what I went through here in setting myself up for retirement, that it all transpired like in fifteen minutes. I was just overwhelmed at how cavalier they go at it here. This university sells itself short in not making a little fuss about some people. This is bad how they do it here, just too darn fast. And I see that not as a criticism because I've been here a long time and I want to remember this place in good terms and they ought to do some work to upgrade themselves. They're selling themselves short here. I think other places do it better. This is fast, casual, incomplete, and they don't go out of their way to cater to you. I say this as what I hope to be a constructive point. I don't think it mattered here nor there for me, but I think it's something they ought to look at here.

More specific suggestions included providing informal retirement seminars or courses. A male oceanographer, aged sixty-seven, from one of the British universities spoke of the value of such informational retirement sessions and how they might work:

> I'm thinking of preretirement courses. I think university people are probably intelligent enough to anticipate these events themselves. Some advice might be to hear the experiences of people who have retired by informal talks. Possibly some of the information could be assimilated for people.

A seventy-year-old male professor of art and art history from the American research university spoke of the need for a preretirement program that would provide knowledge of what lay ahead, in terms of both aging and retirement:

I am really unhappy about the information from the personnel department. They could get some kind of gerontological program going that would include economics and would include some other things. Perhaps that's asking too much of the university. Supposing there were a pamphlet — what you can experience, you know, your kidneys are likely to go, your prostate is going to collapse, and so on. What is the situation in nursing homes? I have a hunch we need to be prepared.

Others also expressed the need for group informational sessions. A male professor of French and Italian, aged sixty-five, from the same university talked about group information sessions that would go beyond financial concerns: "I think they could expand or create a series of conferences of the socio-psychological nature that could help in this transition. What they think are the benefits or prepare some literature. All the information I get is through my wife."

A repeated suggestion from the retirees in both countries was that their colleges and universities should clarify what their status was after retirement. Some spoke poignantly about this issue, revealing both uncertainty and the human concern about loss of status. A sixty-eight-year-old political scientist from the American research university talked of his experience in trying to learn about emeritus status:

There is one thing there, the status of becoming professor emeritus. Most people who retire are interested in that and that carries certain provisions. Now I have been trying to find out — how do I find out about this? First of all, how do you become professor emeritus? I had to find that out. I had to go to my department chairman; I didn't know where to go. What are you entitled to as professor emeritus? It would be nice for them to say, if you want to do this. I had to dig all these things up.

The experience of a seventy-four-year-old male professor of counselor education from the same university, retired for eight years, reflected this continuing concern:

I haven't been able to find out what my obligations are, nor what my prerogatives are as an emeritus professor. For instance, do I have access to the library; is there any problem with my getting access to computer facilities? I don't know that; I don't know whom to contact. I should make it my business to go to the college and find out. On the other hand, the university might have taken the initiative.

British retirees likewise wanted to know about the perquisites that were available to them after retiring. A long-retired eighty-four-year-old man who had taught political theory and institutions at an old civic university put it this way: "The other thing I say is to give you the perquisites or some of the privileges as though you were still a member. The right to use the university sports center, the right to be a member of the club for retired members of the university."

Academics from both countries noted that their universities could do a better job of recognizing them, of keeping in contact with them, and of trying to integrate them into the lives of their academic communities after retirement, as illustrated by this seventy-year-old male British retiree:

Well, they could at least recognize your service. For example, by setting up a tea. Something to recognize you instead of doing nothing like they do here. The university doesn't recognize you; the only people who do are your colleagues. There is very little recognition from the university except a form letter from the registrar.

Similarly, an American university professor of educational psychology, aged sixty-eight, who participated in the transition to retirement study, spoke of what he felt was the loss of community for retirees and their spouses:

There is one thing I have been very concerned about since I have been here. What I think is a great big hole in their personnel policy. I noticed particularly with widows of former staff members who might as well be dead. The minute anyone retires here, that seems to be the end of everything. There is no attempt as near as I can see to make these people still a part of the community. It doesn't bother me because I take the initiative. I would make things for myself. But I have seen a number of people here who have been very lonely and very out of things. Unless they happen to have particular close friends that can form a community, they don't seem to be a part of the university community any longer. That is, they have to depend on the bridges they've built over the years.

When there was recognition and continued contact, it usually came from the retiree's department and was very much appreciated. An eighty-year-old liberal arts college professor of education recalled what his department had done: "I could say what my department did. They gave me a little dinner, a gift, when I left. Sure, I liked that. I think the keeping contact and letting you know that you are one of the ex-members, not completely forgotten, is nice."

Retired academics offered many constructive suggestions for how their college or university could better integrate them into the life of their institution. A male physiologist from the research university, aged sixty-five and about to retire, suggested a handbook that would outline what perquisites were available in retirement:

> I think the university ought to get out a sort of handbook for retirees. So they can learn about a lot of little things that most of them have to learn by hearsay or experience. For example, some retirees don't get on the list of people who can buy tickets to the athletic events. It comes to quite a blow to them if they've been going for years and they don't get their letter and they lose their seating. Quite an important item. Another item is what sort of privileges could a retiree expect in terms of parking on the university campus. They have them, but you have to call and find out about them. That's a little demeaning to have to go in and ask these places would they please put you on the list.

A number of retirees suggested an organization for retired professors that might serve both their intellectual and their social needs. Such retiree organizations can help substitute for the loss of the social as well as mental stimulation of the workplace. A seventy-one-year-old female professor of nursing from the American research university gave her thoughts on this: "I think it would be interesting if the retired faculty had an organization. We could meet and share what's going on in our own professions and we could be in social conversation with others. This would of course be an interdisciplinary group."

Other possible functions of such an organization were suggested by a newly retired male professor of theater, aged sixty-seven, from the same university:

I think faculty members retiring could be used to an advantage if there was some organization set to check with. They don't have to be paid. To use them if they want to do it for whatever. Advice to students, handling a children's company—what would you like to do that we could help you with here at the university? We wouldn't pay you a dime, you're going to get your retirement money and that's what you're going to live on, but is there anything you would like to do that you think you're capable of doing? I think a lot could be gained from people who would have enough energy and interest to spend a little time doing it. I think that kind of organization could use them. It's not a matter of looking for fun; it wouldn't cost them a dime. Except to employ people to do some organizing or coordinating. I think it could happen.

Some retiring professors in the transition to retirement study thought the college or university could be more helpful by providing them with information about important aspects of retirement, such as health and housing, as well as with financial information. A male political scientist, aged seventy, talked about the need for more information about health insurance, which ordinarily undergoes some changes when people retire:

I think they do a pretty good job. I think they should keep the various financial things, insurance and stuff, up to date. I think they should give a very hard look at long-term nursing care insurance. Because that's something I need for myself. That isn't covered by Medicare or Blue Cross. It seems the university should, sometime in the future, set something like that up.

His colleague, a seventy-year-old orthopedic surgeon, had heard of housing assistance that was available from other universities, which he would like to see on his own campus:

The university should do like other universities have been doing and seek provisions to help retirees to move from housing to an apartment. Good apartments are very scarce here. If the university could see that they need apartments, the university could provide them. I've seen a number of people retiring from here moving out of town because they can't find something smaller. You don't need that big house; you need the change into a smaller place. This transition is simply provided by the university.

A final suggestion made by retirees was for the college or university to provide retired academics with continued opportunities for learning. This is obviously of importance to people who have lived by their minds all their lives. Strong feelings about the opportunity to take classes were expressed by an active eighty-six-year-old female liberal arts college musician, who had been retired for more than twenty years and who still gave fifteen music lessons a week:

I know I have friends at Chapel Hill who worked as college professors and they're having a very happy time going back to adult education things, you know. They're in the university. And I think that any college or institution that prepares so-called senior citizen interests would open those channels to the retired people and let them study, such as I have continued. I've grown a great deal. I think I'm a greater, better teacher than I used to be because I've heard everybody that's good! And I've been able to listen and learn. And I think that most retired people need the opportunity to go on learning, don't you? I think it is a fact that anything in the anatomy that you don't use, you lose. It is true. People say to me, I don't know about you, but people have said to me many times, "Your voice is so young." Well, it's because I use it all the time correctly. Whereas [affected voice], "How many nice little old ladies talk like this?" It is just a fact that if you sit, you can't walk. If you don't stretch, you can't breathe. It's all tied up with action, I believe. Use what you have and it will continue to grow and do a considerable more [sic] for you than you realize.

Retiring Gradually or All at Once

The retirement literature suggests that a gradual transition from work to retirement can help ease the transition. This may be because retiring gradually provides a rehearsal for what life in retirement will actually be like. Both academics who had already retired and those who were soon to retire were asked whether they thought it was preferable for a person to retire all at once or more gradually by reducing the number of hours worked. Gradual retirement was preferred to retiring all at once by academics from all types of institutions in the United States and by academics from the British old civic universities. Some retirees, however, said they were undecided on this issue and that the method of retiring depended completely on the individual. A sixty-six-year-old American research university geologist who favored retiring gradually gave his views on how professors could best ease out:

> If I could have gone on half time, I could have taught one class and maybe directed a couple of students, something like that. I think that would be a better circumstance for everyone. Essentially that was the procedure as far as retirement under the rules that existed twenty years ago or so. This would have been attractive to me.

These thoughts were echoed by a male microbiologist, aged sixty-nine, from the same university:

> I think if the university had something of a system, so that you could stay around for a year or two years or so at a reduced workload. "We're going to give you a office and move you over to someplace." I think that would be the type of thing that could be said. I think most people come down to this time and they're not quite sure where they're going to land.

A common theme was that phasing out provided the opportunity to live a more balanced life and spend more time on leisure activities. A male civil engineer from a British university, aged seventy-three, commented on the opportunity gradual retirement offered to develop other interests:

I think that going on working until September 30 and retiring October 1 is thoroughly bad. I think it would be far better to ease people out of work into retirement and make it quite clear that they are not required to be here five days a week or four days a week. Fade them out, give them a chance to develop other interests.

Another British retiree, a male physicist aged sixty-four, gave this advice: "Oh, it's important that you have things to do. If possible, things that you haven't done before. That would be my advice. And don't retire suddenly."

Those academics who had actually had the opportunity to phase out, either formally or informally, like this sixty-two-year-old male economist from the comprehensive university, were usually happy with their decision:

I practiced retirement on a part-time basis. I also, in this part-time process, played around with "Would I be content with a much lower monetary income?" So in a sense this was a preparation for retirement. Knowing that there were things I wanted to do. I was quite pleased with the lowered monetary state and an enriched personal state. In my case I did it gradually because I couldn't finance a break into a single retirement. So in my case I talked them into a circumstance in which I would teach one semester a year, which means four months, and then I would play eight months. I worked one semester, then was off the rest of the year. I did that for about three years before I retired full-time.

A sixty-nine-year-old professor of retailing, also from the comprehensive university, reduced her work hours rather than working fewer months a year:

The year before I retired I asked the dean if I could go on shorter hours. And I went on two-thirds time. And I was going to do that for the year. But at Christmas time the dean came and said, "We need you to teach full-time next semester." So I think that shorter hours, gradually letting out, I assume that the shock might not quite be quite as much as to suddenly have all your time free. I really liked those little bit shorter hours to give me some time to develop ideas of what I wanted to do outside. And it was great, and I would have been very happy to do that all year. You see, I retired before I had to; I had one more year to go. After I had a taste of that two-thirds time, it looked better to me. So when I had to go back on full-time I said, "Fine, but I'm definitely going to retire at the end of this year, then." And I had not made my mind up.

Some academics, like her colleague, a male professor of accounting, aged seventy-four, came up with their own unique method of transitioning to retirement: "I took a one-year leave of absence without pay to explore problems of retirement and to see if I could adjust."

An interesting question raised by some retirees was whether phased retirement might be more beneficial for one sex than the other. Possible gender differences were discussed by a female professor of physical education from the research university, aged sixty-eight, during her preretirement interview:

I think it would depend on a number of things. I think for men it may be desirable to retire by degrees. Well, I think men find it more difficult to retire in some ways than women. It's harder for their wives to have them home all the time. Men have not developed the hobbies lots of times that women have. And they don't have the house to clean. I think it's harder for men to retire because it's harder for them to let go. I think women have had a divided life, professional women lots of times if they have their own home and particularly if they have a family. They've been doing three jobs. It's overwhelming. It's playing a double burden. It's easier for her to lay it down.

These comments suggest that retiring gradually may be helpful in adjusting to the changes in family life that often accompany retirement. A seventy-year-old physician from the same university, who was also about to retire, gave his view on this:

Some people are just going to retire well and other people are going to retire awful. This 10 percent off every year, you know, I think that's a good idea. I think that gets them used to it. What you've got to find out is how it's going to do if you're home all the time with your wife, whom you hardly ever saw.

Although more academics favored retiring gradually than favored retiring abruptly, about one-fourth to one-third of retirees from the various institutions did prefer retiring all at once. This seventy-six-year-old male research university zoologist spoke forcefully against retiring gradually: "A gradual reduction would be a slow throttling off of time, also of funds — your salary would go down. Every time they did this to you it would be an insult and a trauma. You might as well have it; you know it's coming, all at once."

A sixty-six-year-old male British university metallurgist talked of the dangers of hanging on if one retires gradually:

I should think, I'm just guessing though, I should have thought that there is a sense in which it could increase this retirement problem, if there is one. Because as long as you have a part-time interest, you're not making the break. You're just waiting for the three days or so, or whenever you are going to be in. You've got to face it, it's a new phase, so you have to make a new life for yourself. In the business world, I meet a lot of people who are in this sort of position. They usually find they welcome it for a short period, and then they begin to feel, "Well, I don't know, I'd rather go out."

Liberal arts college retirees offered comments similar to those of their university counterparts. A sixty-two-year-old musician described his retirement decision after being offered part-time employment by his college:

For me "all at once" was the only way to do it. I did not want to retire being offered this possibility [gradual retirement] and being urged to do some part-time teaching. I just didn't want to do that. And I know I've talked with others who recently retired and did continue doing some part-time teaching. I wouldn't say they regretted it, but wished that they hadn't done it. Because it just wasn't the same, they just felt that as a part-timer, they were doing this so differently, in connection with their output, with their involvement, and it was so different from when they were full-timers that they didn't enjoy that kind of association.

Attitudes toward Mandatory Retirement

In 1994 the congressional seven-year exemption regarding mandatory retirement in higher education officially ended and mandatory retirement ceased to exist in academe (see National Research Council, *Ending Mandatory Retirement*). Earlier, beginning in 1979, the federal government had extended the mandatory retirement age to seventy. Higher education was granted a temporary exemption from this legislation until 1982. Most of the professors in the transition to retirement study were interviewed after Congress had already extended, but not eliminated, the mandatory retirement age; therefore, they had the option of working later than did the other retirees. Yet most of the respondents in the transition to retirement study, like their colleagues who were interviewed earlier and like most of their colleagues today, chose to retire before the age of seventy. Their reactions to mandatory retirement policies may help shed some light on this retirement decision.

A large majority of academics from all types of institutions in both the United States and the United Kingdom said they felt that mandatory retirement should not be eliminated in higher education. They frequently expressed concerns about the need for intergenerational equity and for "new blood" for their institutions, especially in rapidly changing fields. Implicit and sometimes explicit in their statements was also awareness of the sensitive issue of evaluation of performance in the later stages of the academic career, which the end of mandatory retirement could be expected to bring. A male professor of civic design, aged seventy-five, from a British university talked about the problem of declining abilities as a reason for keeping mandatory retirement: "I cannot see any better solution. People decay and become useless over time; their body presumably does and in academics their judgments do. They become academically useless."

For a female professor of nursing, aged sixty-five, from the American research university there was no point in waiting around for that decline: "I still have my faculties intact. I feel very sorry for people who cling to their work by their fingernails. I want to retire while I'm still flying high."

A common theme was the need to get rid of what some academics saw as "dead wood" in their department or their institution. A seventy-one-year-old male British professor of veterinary science put it this way:

> We have far too much dead wood in many aspects. That's one thing that I haven't mentioned. I serve on the Council of the Veteran Defense Society, which is the organization which undertakes to deal with cases of negligence against members of the profession. Now this is work that I would have never had the time to do before I was retired because it involves a tremendous amount of reading for cases. It brings me back to what I was saying about dead wood because I was slightly horrified when I got on the council, the amount of dead wood that was carried. People who have had very useful ideas but were losing touch, although they all had been extremely able people in their time. But I'm not sure whether we are bringing in a mandatory date of retirement for these, but I think we should be. I am very against dead wood and there are people, after all, in their last few years at the university who are about as useless as they can get. It's very hard to do. There is a lot of dead wood around and therefore I am in favor of a mandatory retirement age because while some people may still be able to make a valuable contribution, you must get rid of the ones that can't. I'm sorry I'm very hard about this, but one's main duty, after all, is to students in academic life.

A male British professor of child health, aged sixty-eight, spoke to the critical issue of turnover in academe, of the need to make room for young people who need jobs:

> I think on balance, yes. I've seen it in other aspects, in my work on this committee I've been referring to. There were occasions where an individual came up to a certain age, which was the age for retirement, and they wanted to go on and in certain circumstances one should advise this should happen. On the other hand, one has to think, if you let someone go for rather longer, it may make a block on the ladder for people coming up. There are all sorts of things one has to think about in this context. So that's why I say on balance, if you have a set retiring age, it swings around the balance. It evens itself out.

The words of a sixty-eight-year-old American research university zoologist summed up the views of many of his colleagues regarding mandatory retirement: "It is probably a good way to clear the books, so you can bring in young blood, and we need young blood."

The thoughtful comments of a sixty-eight-year-old male professor of education and psychology from the same institution expressed how complex the end of mandatory retirement age could be both for institutions of higher education and for professors themselves:

> It would cause all sorts of dissension to not have a mandatory retirement date. To say, "So and so is teaching; I had to retire." I don't believe anybody is wise enough to pick out the people that can and the people that can't. I don't think anybody is wise enough.

Other academics, like this seventy-year-old male historian from the United Kingdom, felt that even the present mandatory retirement age was too high:

> Frankly, I would lower it. It would make possible the better adjustment to the life of retirement. My feeling is that sixty-five is plenty late enough for a chap to retire with a good prospect on life. In any case, there is the fairness one has to feel due to the oncoming generations. I think that is important. I think it's fair enough. One has to think about the well-being of the craft to which one belongs. For me, history.

Although there were fewer voices favoring the elimination of mandatory retirement than for keeping it, those academics who did favor its elimination spoke mainly of the importance of allowing productive older faculty to be able to continue their work. They believed that distinguished professors should be able to continue to contribute to their institutions and to the larger society. A sixty-nine-year-old professor of English from the American research university expressed his view in the strongest words: "The university ought to fire more people for incompetence and occasionally keep the distinguished. I know some people on this faculty who are living in a university welfare state, who ought to go."

Others, like this male professor of journalism, aged eighty-one, from the same institution, pointed out that what sometimes happens is that older faculty choose to move to another college or university primarily because of the mandatory retirement age:

I think it should be based upon the individual case. Because there are a lot of men who are able to work, and they have a good deal to offer. I wanted to stay on here. I tried every way I could to get them to alter the rules so I could stay, but they wouldn't do it. I even talked to the president of the university one time. Some of them told me that they thought eventually the rule would be changed, but not in time to help me. So I had to leave. Another university got me.

A British male psychologist, aged seventy-four, agreed that some academics should be asked to stay on, at the same time conveying the often harsh impact an abrupt cutoff could have on people:

I think I would say no [to eliminating mandatory retirement]. I think this is partly conditioned by what happened to me. There were so many small jobs offered that I was never put on the shelf by anyone. When I say sharp cutoff I mean that when you retire, you give up everything that relates to your professorship and nobody asks you to do any more, anywhere. To make it mandatory in that sense, when you're not asked to do any more, then it's brutal. And it may be like this in some other departments, and then it makes retirement very, very difficult.

Summing it all up, a sixty-four-year-old professor of physical education from a liberal arts college spoke of the enormous complexity of the issues raised by the end of mandatory retirement. This seemed to be on the minds of many of her fellow academics across colleges and universities.

Do I think that they should absolutely cut out at seventy? No. I'll tell you, that's hard, because some people age sooner than others, and some people really ought to retire, and there are others who are good until they're seventy-five and eighty. But some of these people haven't got sense enough to quit, that's the trouble. Well, I think that there should be a mandatory requirement at a certain age, yes, I do. Even though it's a personal thing with some people. Yeah, I'm thinking of the college part of it. Some people just aren't any good after a certain age. They should have sense enough to quit. But sometimes they don't, so then I suppose you have to have a rule. You take, for instance, Janet O'Conner; she will never quit. What are you going to do in a case like that? The college is kind of helpless. I'm thinking of the college, because I think some people just can't carry on. Students are paying dearly for their education, and I think they deserve the best.

Staying or Leaving:
Where to Live

"I have my home here. I wouldn't consider leaving."

a seventy-one-year-old female professor of nursing

"I think once you leave the university setup and once you leave

the students, it's time to leave."

a seventy-one-year-old professor of art and art history

Deciding where to live in retirement is important for older persons because it affects all aspects of their retirement lifestyle: their social networks, activities, financial well-being, and access to health care. As noted previously, most retirees across occupational groups choose to grow old in place. This is primarily because of long-standing ties and established associations in their preretirement community. For those persons who do choose to move to another community, there are both the challenges and the opportunities of a new environment.

The majority of the retired academics continued to live in their preretirement communities after retiring. There were some differences, however, among retirees from the different types of institutions and between British and American academics. Retirees from the American research university were most likely to stay in their preretirement community after retiring (73 percent), whereas retirees from the British universities were least likely to stay after retiring (56 percent). Retirees from the American comprehensive university and the liberal arts colleges fell between those retirees, with 61 percent and 69 percent, respectively, continuing to live in their preretirement communities. These differences in staying or leaving after retirement may have reflected the residential community where the college or university was located more than they did institutional affiliation or national differences. Both the American comprehensive university and the British old civic universities were located in cities of several hundred thousand population or more; the American research university and the liberal arts colleges, in contrast, were located in either small towns or small cities that offered such amenities as a bucolic setting, convenient access to the college or university, low crime rates, good transportation, good medical care, and a moderate cost of living. These amenities are much sought after by retired people. Additionally, the British universities were located reasonably close to seaside and Lake District retirement communities, which helped make retirement migration an attractive and viable option.

Why They Stayed

The most frequent reasons the retired academics gave for deciding to stay in their preretirement communities were personal and reflected attachment to people and to place: this was where the retiree's home was; this was where family and, more frequently, friends and colleagues were; these were the kind of people they knew and enjoyed. Although most of the retired academics had come to the college or university community because of their jobs, as time passed they began to perceive that community as their permanent home. In the interview, the academics were asked, "At the time of your retirement, did you consider leaving your community?" The strong response of a male research university orthopedist, aged sixty-nine, was typical of those who would not consider leaving their preretirement community and chose to remain in place:

> I did not. I wouldn't even give it a thought. In fact, we have given positive thinking to not wanting to leave. Because this is home; we

have roots here. We have family roots, we have friendship roots, and I also have professional roots. And we're comfortable. We're permitted by staying here to live the kind of life we've built up all these years and have gotten accustomed to, and we want it to continue as long as possible. Like an old shoe.

Both males and females expressed these feelings of attachment to place. A seventy-one-year-old female nursing professor from the research university said: "Well, I have my home here. I wouldn't consider leaving, because I've lived here the longest of any place I've ever lived in my life. There's no place else I'd want to go." A sixty-six-year-old male mathematician from one of the liberal arts colleges said: "My roots are too deep here. I know the community pretty well so far and the people. It's a good place to be. If I had to do everything over, I would do it again."

For a few retirees, their preretirement community had always been home; this community was where their origins were, where they had grown up, where they had lived their lives. A liberal arts college musician, aged seventy-nine, said:

My roots are very deep here. My father went into business here in 1890. He took his bride to our house in 1891. We lived in that house until I moved out of it to move here, which was a matter of sixty-six years. My roots were very deep here. I don't think I would have considered going anywhere else.

Two male British academics, a seventy-four-year-old physician and an eighty-seven-year-old political theorist, showed this same attachment to place of origin:

One reason was that for many years we had been in the family house that my grandfather built in 1900. So it didn't really arise. I suppose I just stayed here because I really didn't think of going anywhere else.

Because my wife was born here. This is where we live. We decided to keep the house; then later we decided it would be much more sensible to get a small flat. And more sensible to live where she was born, where she knew people, where all her relatives are from.

Some retirees, although identifying their preretirement community as the one where they chose to remain after retiring, decided to remain there for only part of the year, while maintaining a second home elsewhere for several months each year. One of these "part-leavers" was a seventy-eight-year-old male research university periodontist:

I went to Hawaii two years in a row. This time I'm going back down to where I was reared, down to the Gulf Coast of Mississippi. I'm going to where the Little Biloxi enters the Big Biloxi. That's why I haven't bought a place. If I just have a home where I used to work, I can leave at any time. You see, the snow and primarily the ice. I fell last December and hurt my neck and it still bothers me. I go fishing, visit friends I have from the navy.

Another retiree, a research university pharmacist aged seventy-five, shared the desire of many retirees to escape the northern winters, but not to leave his preretirement community permanently:

Well, we have a very comfortable home where we are. We live in a lovely neighborhood. We have nice neighbors, and we thought perhaps if we could go away in the colder months of the year, it might be nice to be part of this university, which has many things to offer culturally, academically. We go to Arizona, though we have been to Florida. I do considerable reading, exercise, travel, a little golf.

An eighty-year-old periodontist had a more complex pattern of yearly moves, but always came back to his preretirement community for part of the year:

We planned to keep our home because our family is here. Our daughters live here. We'll always come back to this place. We leave for Arizona in the winter for four months and live in the travel trailer park. We leave our trailer there. In the summer we go to Estes Park in the Rocky Mountains and live in our cabin. In the spring and the fall we return here. That's the result of long-term planning. We drive a car on the trips.

Many academics spoke of their preretirement community as the place where their friends or family were. Two single British female academics, a seventy-eight-year-old from the faculty of education and a seventy-four-year-old from the department of psychology, talked about the importance of those ties in their lives:

> My friends live here. If I went anywhere else, I would go into a place where I didn't know anybody and I would have to start from scratch. I have no particular interest in doing that. I wasn't concerned to go to the east side or to the country. I'm very comfortable here. Things are pretty pleasant, really. I didn't see any point in moving. I was interested in people here and things here and so there's no point in moving.

> Family was part of it. Some part of it is, if I stay here there are people that I know to begin with. It's up to me how much I keep in touch with my colleagues in the department. As it happens, I have kept in touch. I didn't want to go to a new place and have to start from scratch and make new friends.

These thoughts conveying attachment to people were expressed by males as well as females, marrieds as well as singles, and American as well as British retirees. A married male American research university physician, aged seventy-seven, gave his opinion: "It's foolish to leave. There is good medical care here, friends here. It's foolish to break ties. I think it's foolish to retire and leave your own environment."

Some retirees who moved from their preretirement communities after retiring missed their long-established social contacts and thought seriously about returning to those communities. A sixty-eight-year-old research university psychiatrist, who had left his university community for new job opportunities elsewhere, talked of his experience: "As I wind down more, with less contacts on the professional level, there is perhaps a need to be in a location where your friends are. My friends are mostly where I used to live. There are values there that are not here."

Other academics toyed with the idea of migrating after retiring, but rejected it. A British dentist, aged seventy-seven, was one who had considered leaving, but in the end decided to remain in his preretirement community, citing the negative experiences of other academics who had left the community and consequently lost their social circle:

Well, there's an immediate feeling you ought to go to some lovely place in the country or by the coast. Your whole life and your interests are around the area you work. There's a lot of considerations before you go to some strange place, at an age where you will find it difficult to make friends easily. You've got to start again and I don't think it would be easy. So many people I've known have returned or come back. We sat down and thought about it and had this initial urge to go. People down there wanted us to go and then I said, "No, be sensible." Our interests, our friends, are around here. We can always go to these places for a holiday. We can go in the summer.

Proximity to family could be a powerful motivator to remain in the preretirement community. A British physiologist, aged sixty-eight, put his reason for staying succinctly: "For one reason only. I've got my daughter and three grandchildren here." Another British retiree in child health, aged seventy-four, also talked about family factors in his decision not to move to a new community:

Many years before we retired, my wife and I used to go to the Lake District a lot. I've always known the Lake District very well. I think we always had sort of an idea in the back of our mind that we'd like to retire to the lakes. But when I retired, she had already been ill for two years. Despite being ill, she was still working. Consequently, there wasn't any question of our moving. Even if she'd been well, I don't think we would have moved. I've got one branch of my family here as well. I've got a daughter that lives here. That's another reason why I wouldn't want to go.

An American liberal arts college Spanish professor, aged seventy, would have liked to leave his college community, but did not because of family reasons: "I would like to move to the South, but I can't. For family reasons I won't do it. My wife likes this weather, you know, the winter. And we have a daughter here too. It's out of the question."

Some academics chose to remain in place not because other family members actually lived in the same community, but because their preretirement community was located conveniently enough for family members to be able to visit them. A sixty-seven-year-old research university professor said that it was important for him to live within easy commuting distance of his children: "This is 'home' to our kids. We have two sons in Omaha who like to come home here."

Employment of spouses also influenced whether to stay in place or to leave. More and more, when the husband and the wife are both working, one spouse, usually the younger, may continue to work after the older spouse retires. This was the case for a research university religion professor, aged sixty-five, and a liberal arts college geology professor, aged eighty, both of whom had wives who were still employed:

> For the immediate present, she is the executive librarian at the Law College. She's about five or six years younger than I am. Somewhere in there. I have no idea how much longer she's going to work. You know, when she retires, I'm sure we'll stay here; we have our own house.

> Certainly an important factor for us was my wife's situation as a private teacher and as a teacher at the community college, and her work as an organist. All of these have gone beyond retirement; they have no mandatory retirement at her college. So she's still on the faculty at eighty. This question just doesn't come up. You sign the contract and go on.

The death or illness of a spouse can also affect the decision of where to live after retiring. For some, frailty or death of a partner may result in what has often been called a spoiled retirement, with plans that had been made jointly now changed or abandoned. This is what happened to a sixty-nine-year-old research university pediatrician after his wife's death:

> At the time when my wife was still alive, we planned to retire to Switzerland. We had an apartment there. We had many friends there. She grew up there; I grew up there. But now, alone, I have no interest, and I have good friends here. And I like to travel; I go once or twice a year to Europe. So I decided to stay here.

In addition to the advantages of home, friends, and family, another reason for choosing to remain in their preretirement community was what many of the retirees saw as the considerable advantages it offered. Many of the academics said they would find these advantages difficult to duplicate elsewhere. Two research university professors, a male social worker, aged sixty-five, and a female physical educator, aged sixty-eight, described why they wanted to stay in their preretirement community:

This is a community of a nice size, not too big, yet big enough to have shopping and other advantages. Perhaps among the largest reasons are the cultural advantages, the culture of the university. So a fairly small town and a big university. I'm just happy to be here.

We'll probably buy a house in Florida, and we'll go down there for the winter. Our permanent residence will remain here. A college town is a marvelous place for retirement. I think maybe you feel like I do when the college kids are gone; we breathe a sigh of relief and we can go downtown and park. But the town wouldn't be the same without them and you're always glad to see them coming back. And there are things to do. We have community theater, there are lots of clubs, there are lots of opportunities for volunteer work. There's so much you can do. It's just a fine place to retire. It's a balanced community.

Similarly, a seventy-seven-year-old British materials scientist spoke of the cultural advantages of his much larger city: "It offers an enormous amount of an interesting realm of the arts. There's all sorts of things that are far more convenient here than other places."

For a number of retirees, like this seventy-one-year-old female professor of nursing, the advantages of a university medical center were important: "I stayed around here because I had good connections with medical and dental care. I stayed here also because of the activities that go on here, the activities of a university community. But it was mainly the health care that kept me here." Her male colleague, also from the American research university, said: "It's foolish to leave. There is good medical care here. I think it's foolish to retire and leave your own environment."

British retirees, like this anatomist, aged seventy-five, likewise spoke of the importance of good medical care in deciding to remain in their preretirement community:

> I thought I would like to live in Wales and I nearly bought a house, but then I wasn't very well again, about two or three years before retiring. And I had known people here and I thought, "Thank goodness I'm here," and I'm not leaving. Medically, I'm thankful to live here. That's one thing.

The availability of college and university facilities such as libraries was an important factor for some academics in deciding to remain in their preretirement community. This was one of the reasons given by two British retirees, a seventy-five-year-old psychologist and a seventy-six-year-old architect, both males:

> One of the essentials is that I should be near a good library. I couldn't retire into the country where I wouldn't be near books. The library is available here. That's one reason. The other thing is that we've got a lot of friends in this area. This city is a scrappy place in some ways, but there are a lot of things we like, concerts, theatres, and other things of that kind. There are quite a lot of interesting things going on here. We like the area very much and we don't see any reason why we should move. We have family in the area, too.

> The experiences I've had with other people who have retired and disappeared has been disastrous for them. It cuts you off from the libraries, it cuts you off from activities that you have been involved with. My wife and I decided that it would be a total mistake to disappear into the countryside. We would rather go to the countryside for a short time but still be able to come back.

Some academics spoke of the continued professional opportunities their college or university offered them in retirement as a major reason for deciding to stay in their preretirement community. A seventy-one-year-old home economist from the research university talked about opportunities that had developed for her in another college of her home university:

I knew what I wanted to do, and I wanted to finish up the job that I hadn't had a chance to finish up. I'm not saying that I'll always stay here; I don't really know. What I'm doing is really an extension of what I was doing before. I really felt I didn't have time to finish up the kind of thing that needed to be done, that should have been done during the years that I was teaching. Well, you see, I've taught for many years a course to the dental students, and it was only a theory course, and I never really had the chance to demonstrate how to put it to work. In other words, the practical aspects of it. I always wanted to go over to the college, but there was never any time. I could have done that or research in the college. What I'm doing is working in a preventive dentistry program in a nutrition counseling program. We've got a program started that's rather a new program, and I'm in the periodontics department. Patients who go through our program have both the nutritional aspects of it and the other aspects of it. And what we're really doing is helping the dental students, and we're supervising the teaching of the students.

A seventy-eight-year-old musician from the comprehensive university also had found opportunities for professional work in his pre-retirement community:

I wanted to carry on with my work and so did my wife. We weren't working nearly as hard, of course. It would be very difficult at my age to find a community that was very interested in music. For that very reason, the problem of getting started again. You just couldn't organize a class without contacts. I'm very well known here and I wouldn't have been in any other place. I would have probably wanted to go south if I was willing to move anywhere. It's always filled with people who are retired and wanting to do things.

A research university botanist, aged seventy-one, noted the continuing opportunities available for him as a laboratory scientist: "My work is here; I'm settled here. The laboratory, library, and equipment are here. The freedom to work as you want is here. A good atmosphere for work is here."

Scientists from the United Kingdom had similar reactions to professional opportunities available to them in their preretirement community. A male pathologist, aged eighty-three, said: "Because the opportunities for work are continuing here. The opportunities for beginning straight away were here; we didn't have to sit around and decide where shall we move to." A male physician, aged seventy-six, said: "I couldn't work in London near as well as I do here. I've been here thirty years and I'm organized here at home and at the university. I like it here. I enjoy the trip to London. I love living here. I wouldn't dream of moving during retirement."

Most of the reasons retirees gave for continuing to live in their preretirement communities reflected the considerable personal attractions of those communities as places to live. A less positive reason for remaining was that retirees felt they could not afford to move or, at the very least, that it was more financially advantageous not to move. While no more than 5 percent of the retired academics from any type of institution gave financial constraints as a reason for staying in their preretirement communities, for those retirees financial factors were important in deciding where to live. A seventy-one-year-old British university retiree from the faculty of education discussed why he stayed:

There are local advantages in retiring in your local area such as special concessions for pensioners. You wouldn't necessarily get the same concessions on travel in any town. I can't get concessions in London, where I used to live and work, but I can here. It's very convenient and worth quite a lot. I can travel into the city for nine pence — if I get the right bus.

His colleague, a male mathematician, aged sixty-six, also talked about large regional differences in the cost of living in the United Kingdom:

The other thing, of course, there is a financial factor. It's one of the areas of the country [northern England] where houses are relatively cheap. If I were to think of moving, say to the London area or the south coast, I couldn't. The house I've got here is so much more modest than in those areas. It's not a simple matter on the financial side to move out of this city. I gave a piece of advice to my boys to buy the best possible house that they can afford.

This male American liberal arts college musician, aged sixty-eight, likewise found it difficult financially to move to a more expensive part of the country: "I was ready to buy a house in Westfield [New Jersey], but the cost was so enormous. I didn't know if it was worthwhile. It was just a financial matter; otherwise, I wouldn't have stayed here at all. I still might move if I find an apartment where I want to be."

Generally, the American liberal arts college retirees had lower incomes than did their university counterparts, which probably affected their ability to move after retirement. One of those liberal arts colleges retirees, an eighty-seven-year-old mathematician who had been retired for more than two decades, came immediately to the point when he was asked why he remained in his preretirement community: "No money."

Why They Left

Some academics left their preretirement communities, but many who left wished to retain ties to those communities and not be completely cut off from long-standing professional and social relationships. A research university mathematician, aged seventy-two, communicated his desire to enjoy what he saw as the best of both worlds—to move to a new community after retiring, but also to maintain ties by coming back occasionally to visit people in his former university community:

Sometimes when I go back, you know, I think of the fact that if I lived here it would be easy to get over to the library. But then once again, I'm sort of glad that I am living away from the university and can go back to the university and visit with friends. We are in much more contact the few days I'm there, I think, than if I lived here. Even teaching in a university, that becomes humdrum and routine. What a person wants to do is to get out and be involved in things which are perhaps beyond your own training. When I visit the people in the math department, we sit around and shoot the breeze so to speak, but we talk about mathematics too as well. I kind of like that because that group and I, we're not related but we have a lot in common. A lot of experiences in common and it's fun to review those experiences. The interaction now is more concentrated because I stay only a few days there. When I go back I usually have my questions pretty much put together before I leave here. Well, if I lived there, the questions would come up, but would be spread over a greater length of time.

Academics chose to leave their preretirement communities for a variety of reasons, including the wish to be nearer to family or friends, a better climate, return to their hometown, and desire for new professional opportunities. Personal reasons for leaving their college or university community were given more frequently than were professional reasons. For example, this seventy-eight-year-old research university dentist chose to return to his hometown: "It is my wife's and my hometown. We started preparing for it nine years before retirement." Sometimes returning home also meant being closer to other family members, as was true for this comprehensive university education professor, aged sixty-seven:

> One of the main reasons was we'd been out here on vacation a number of times and of course, being a native Oregonian, it was coming home. A number of my relatives still live here in the state, my brother and sister. Those were basic considerations. I just wasn't being thrown out to a strange territory at all. We still have quite close contacts with relatives that live on the other side of the state, but they come over rather frequently.

Academics from all institutions and from both countries spoke of the desire to be near family members, especially their grown children and grandchildren, as they grew older. Many of them, like this male liberal arts college economist, aged eighty-eight, moved great distances to achieve their desire: "Because my kids live here [the West Coast]. They live out here and we came to be near them. We have four grandchildren in Seattle and one here."

A seventy-one-year-old English professor from the research university moved with his wife to the East Coast for the same kind of reasons:

I would say the most important thing is to choose his location carefully, and it would have to be what his wife enjoys too, and in terms of his relationship to his family, assuming that those relations are warm. I have four children and my relations and those of my wife are very warm, so the family means a great deal to us. And being in the East we are closer to them.

Unmarried retirees without children or grandchildren, like this research university home economist, aged eighty-eight, also chose to be near relatives, in this case her sister: "Because my family is so scattered and there's so many interesting things to see. I was alone and I had family in other areas."

But there were also caveats about moving to where grown children or other relatives lived. The major concern expressed by the retired academics was that they might intrude into the lives of their grown children. A sixty-seven-year-old professor of preventive medicine from the research university related his experience:

Lots of people have been successful in leaving the community where they've spent so many years. Looking back on it, I question whether that's a real wise move. And even in our instance, where our children and family were all out here, I'm not too sure that's the wisest thing that we did. You can very easily come out and spend three or four months in the winter out there, and that suffices pretty well. You kind of feel that you become a drag on the younger people. It'd be a lot better if I could just come out and visit, then go back or go someplace else. It just seems to me that might be a more pleasant way to do it. What happens to you as you become older is that you have the feeling that they should devote more time to you. Your family doesn't look on you as being that much of a contribution to the whole thing. Oh, sure, you can help them do some little odds and ends occasionally, but they have no big ongoing thing. They're both salaried people and they have no big ongoing thing that you can contribute to. You need to hold onto something that you can kind of make a daily contribution on.

To me, there isn't anything worse than a day with absolutely nothing to do.

Concern about moving to where families were was also expressed by a male liberal arts college musician, aged seventy-seven: "We do not advise, particularly, the families going where their families are, because I think there is an obligatory situation."

A nonfamily reason that academics gave for leaving their preretirement community was to find professional opportunities elsewhere. Often this meant employment at another institution where they were permitted to work, usually on a year-by-year basis, beyond the mandatory retirement age. A male comprehensive university education professor, long retired and now ninety, summed it up: "The main reason I left was I got a job teaching in South Carolina." Others, like this eighty-year-old male journalism professor from the research university, talked about their desire to continue working over the long term:

> Well, I knew I was coming up for retirement, so I started looking for another job. About the time that I quit the university, I had the job at another university. And I taught there for another five years. I retired when I was seventy-three. If we [he and his wife] hadn't encountered this health problem, I'd probably still be teaching. Because I am still in pretty good health and still very active. They were hiring me on an annual basis. I've seen too many old men quit work and sit down and die.

Academics who were in professions that involved direct practice with clients or patients could often find professional opportunities elsewhere, as did this male research university surgeon, aged seventy, who was working at a community hospital in another part of the country:

> When I was looking ahead to retirement, maybe ten years before, I came out to California and took the state board licensure exams. I got my California license long before I ever had any idea of how it would work out or would fit in. So this was a form of planning, I think. As it turned out, it was the best thing I ever did. When we came here, we were all set up, no problem in getting a license.

Whereas things are getting tougher all the time, so many doctors. There wasn't any question about it. I had an opportunity to go into practice here with someone I knew and become associated with him in an established practice. So, rather than just sit there and pass up this opportunity which might never come again, with a little pushing from my wife, I went.

Some academics, like this seventy-year-old business professor, sought professional opportunities elsewhere because of lack of material support for work after retirement in their preretirement community:

You see, if they gave emeritus profs satisfactory office space, I would certainly want to have a base here and spend part of the year, and be elsewhere part of the year, because there are some activities I cannot pursue here. There's an office here right down the hall with half a dozen names, and they cram them in there, half a dozen of them, in a broom closet, and this is what they give you here. It's bad. Other schools, some of them, do very well. So I won't go in there, so I won't have an office here and I won't stay here. I won't keep a residence here because of the same reason, because of no office. I have all my life had a home in Portland. It is out there and I can use it as a legal residence and as a base. I am going to keep working. Workwise, I will be working in Texas and in Washington, D.C.

Like many retirees from other occupational groups, some of the academics wanted to move to a better climate when they retired. Retirement migration was usually to the Sunbelt states of the United States or to the seashore or Lake District regions of the United Kingdom. For a male research university speech professor, aged seventy-four, the destination was Florida:

We went there primarily because we had gone to a convention in Miami. We had gone through Sarasota then and just fell in love with the town. Beyond that, at the time of my retirement, my son was teaching at the University of Florida so we said that would be close enough so we could see him occasionally and still not be in his hair or he in ours. We no sooner moved to Sarasota than he moved to Arizona. It's a lovely place. It's not too large. And my doctor advised me to get out of the cold climate.

For his colleague in engineering, a seventy-three-year-old male from the same university, the destination was Arizona:

It was getting pretty cold in the winter. So I have this job at Colorado State. Change is good. I have lots of friends there, including many who came from the Midwest. I value the professional contacts that come from the summer job [in Colorado]. This way I coast all winter and work in the summer again. I live in Arizona eight months a year and four months a year in Colorado. My residence is here [Arizona], of course. We visited down here a number of times; there was really nothing tying us any more to the Midwest. I would say the main reason was climate.

A male liberal arts college musician, aged seventy-seven, chose New Mexico:

We were just ready to retire. We had made up our minds during that period of five years or so, and we were discussing things that we would like to go somewhere else. We were glad we did. We were glad for a number of reasons. We were thinking of the change of climate, which we've certainly had here. It's really been a delightful place to live and I don't think we would discourage anyone from coming here. In fact, some of our friends have been talking about it because they've been here to visit and like it so much. We felt the humidity in the Mississippi Valley there was very oppressive.

A few academics, like this male comprehensive university social scientist, aged seventy-one, chose to live in planned retirement communities in the western part of the United States:

My city is a very good town in the Midwest to live, but the weather is very bad. I do not believe in hanging around a college campus after you retire. I've seen that at Kansas State University, in Manhattan, Kansas. I lived there. You see these old ghosts walking around the campus. It's the most pitiful thing I've seen. And besides, you come out here to Leisure World and the Long Beach area here, that's where you meet all your friends. The club from my state is the largest club in Leisure World.

Some retirees migrated to better climates primarily for health reasons, as did this liberal arts college professor of religion, now eighty-eight and living on his own:

In 1967 my medical doctor told me I had a bad case of asthma and that I must go to Tucson, Arizona. In 1969 we moved here permanently, and I am told that I must remain here all the rest of my life. Asthma, as you know, cannot be cured — but, thank God, it can be controlled. Of course, you know that my dear Abigail died in 1972. I do not like to live alone, but keep up my reading and writing and make the best of things. As you will note in the questionnaire, I am happy and content. As long as I can take care of myself, I will not complain.

A final reason for leaving the preretirement community was verbalized by a few retirees, but may have been on the minds of more. The comments of these retirees reflected feelings of loss of status and of no longer being part of the life of their college or university. A seventy-one-year-old art and art history professor talked about why he had left his university community:

We built a house about twenty-five years ago on the Cape and went back there every summer. And I think once you leave the university setup and once you leave the students, it's time to leave. It's quite different. You can't really be on the outside and still be a part of the university. It doesn't work that way. It's certainly a great place to be for a lot of people. I liked it too, but I like this place better. You're not needed really by the university once you retire; you're just out of it. And that's exactly what happened.

In order to avoid these problems, a male research university musician, aged seventy-one, had made a calculated decision to move immediately upon retiring:

To me, life is a wonderful adventure and I can't see sitting down and closing the books on your last ten years and look out of the house and wish you had a job. I just feel that one of the best things was to move out of town the day we were through, and that's what we did. It's over, those years. This wasn't a sudden thing. We had thought about this for a long time; we had watched a lot of our friends retire. I've seen a lot of people retire. And I've seen a lot of people becoming morose. I think I know what resident faculties feel about their older people. I didn't want to be under anybody's feet. I didn't want that kind of life. I didn't want to be put out to pasture.

Others who were not yet retired, like this sixty-nine-year-old writer, planned the same course of action. For him, a new life beckoned in retirement:

I do feel that it's time for me to move on. I'm looking for another era, another productive era in my life, and so the change is welcome to me. I love it here; I think it's Shangri-La in many ways, but I don't particularly want to hang around here without my job to do. That seems to me to be depressing. I would rather move to a new community and establish a new non–"has been" status for myself.

Experiencing Retirement

"The sun still shone."

a seventy-four-year-old male professor of German

Like other important transitions in the life course — marriage, the birth of a child, or children leaving home — retirement can be mainly a positive or a negative experience. Research shows that most people adjust well to retirement and enjoy it; however, as many as one-third may experience problems in making this adjustment, and a small minority of people never adjust. A number of factors affect how well people will adapt to this new phase of life, including their attitude toward retirement, health, financial status, social involvements, marital status, and the meaning of their life's work. Generally, people with a positive attitude toward retirement who enjoy good health, adequate financial resources, and continued social contacts and activity will make a good adjustment to retirement.

Retired academics from all institutions in both nations were far more positive than negative about retirement. This is not to say that negative views about retirement were not expressed; they were — and often vociferously. However, approximately 40 percent of retirees from all institutions said there were no negative aspects at all about their retirement; in contrast, only a handful of retirees said there were no positive aspects of their retirement.

I looked at satisfaction of retired academics in a number of ways: by all measures, the academics were generally quite satisfied with their lives in retirement. For example, retirees in the research university transition to retirement study reported extremely high levels of life satisfaction after the first year of retirement, when one might have expected some strong negative reactions to their new life situation. Those academics scored an average (mean) of 88.8 on a 100-point scale asking them to rate how satisfied they were with their life in general. What is more, the life satisfaction ratings of those recently retired academics increased slightly from their preretirement average life satisfaction score (85.9). Among academics who had been retired for longer periods, two-thirds of the liberal arts college and comprehensive university retirees also scored high on a 90-point life satisfaction index. Moreover, the vast majority of British retirees, when asked to respond to specific questions regarding satisfaction on this same index, said they were just as happy as when they were younger, things they did were as interesting to them as they ever were, and they were satisfied when they looked back on their lives. What is more, 93 percent of those British retirees disagreed with the statement "This is the dreariest time of my life."

The comments of retired academics in the American research university longitudinal transition to retirement study are particularly telling because they show how retirees react to and deal with a major recent change in their lifestyle. In their postretirement interview one year after retirement, those academics were asked, "All things considered, how have you found the first year of retirement to be?" About three-fourths of the retirees said they were quite positive about the first year of retirement; in fact, some said that retirement was even better than they had expected it to be. Others (about 8 percent) commented on how busy retirement had been so far. Another 5 percent said retirement was as good as could be expected, and about the same percent said they noticed no difference because they had continued their preretirement work involvements. In contrast, only a small percentage of the retired academics expressed negative feelings about retirement; for example, 4 percent said they felt ignored and 2 percent expressed concerns about having to establish a new routine. The majority of academics, like this male musician, aged sixty-nine, and female instructional designer, aged seventy-one, were quite enthusiastic about retirement:

> I've loved every minute of it! It took me about thirty minutes to adjust to it, and since then I've been deliriously happy. Each day is a new experience; you can plan to do exactly what you wish to. I haven't retired really from music at all; I've just retired from paperwork and answering the telephone and doing all the routine things that after a while get a little tedious because you've done them so many times that they no longer offer any challenge to you. Now I'm completely free; I can accept any and all invitations; and so that's exactly what I'm doing.

> I am trying to think of some words to describe it. I have very positive feelings about it. I've been to the West Coast and to the East Coast and to the Gulf visiting my children and friends, so I've been able to travel and see my family and friends and that's been great. And I've found a group here in town, the local cable programmers, working on cable [television], and they were organizing last year. So I've gotten involved with them and it's mutually beneficial, I guess. They seem to like me very much. It is, of course, the visualization I'm very much interested in.

There were a few retirees who were pleasantly surprised because retirement was even better than they had anticipated. A sixty-six-year-old female rhetoric professor and a seventy-year-old political scientist shared this reaction:

> I'd say better than I expected it to be. In a lot of ways, the pleasures are more acute. There's almost a sense of adolescence; everything can happen; all sorts of nice things. It's lovely to get up in the morning and not have to rush off, especially during the bad weather; you get right up from the breakfast table and instead of doing dishes and picking up, you can go leave. And that's sinfully indulgent. I enjoy the guilt.

> It's better than I thought. I've enjoyed it. And I've had, as far as I can see, no serious problems. It's been pretty easy because I have had no financial problems; I have had no health problems that I

haven't had before. I've been much busier than I thought I'd be. And I've been able to do some things that I wanted to do. It's been a very good year; I'm now a grandparent!

Others, like this sixty-nine-year-old education professor, noted both the satisfactions and adjustments of retirement:

Well, we've found a lot of satisfactions and there were also some major adjustments to make. And I guess I anticipated a year ago that I would feel unemployed, I wouldn't be able to organize my time, I wouldn't have enough to do to keep me busy. You know, when you are teaching, you have to organize your time, you have to be in class a certain time, you have to prepare your lectures, and so forth. And, of course, attend committee meetings, and all that. And I anticipated that I would have too much free time and not enough commitments to keep me on schedule. But this hasn't happened quite that way. I've found plenty to do, and I've written more nasty letters to the editor than before. I've been on the television and the radio a few times. I've also continued to serve the university. I've written a correspondence study manual more efficiently than I ever could have before. I've also remained on dissertation committees. I did anticipate that I would miss students, but I do have contact with them.

For some, like this sixty-six-year-old nursing professor, retirement was not what she had planned because family illness and caregiving intervened:

Fine, but not entirely like we planned. The thing that we hadn't planned was that about the time that I retired my mother was recovering from a serious illness and, you know, she's eighty-five years old and could no longer take care of herself. So she's living with us now. So that altered, for instance, our volunteer work, and that we've set aside because of her care.

Some academics were initially negative about retirement, but became more positive as their first year of retirement went on. An art professor, aged seventy-one, recounted his experience:

Fine, after I took a trip abroad and that changed my perspective. Because I did what I wanted to do and saw things at a time when I wanted to see them, and it was at my own pace and doing what I wanted to. Before the trip abroad I was feeling resentful, because the retirement had not been my choice, and the fact that it was not my choice affected the way I felt about it. But after taking advantage of the possibilities of not having to teach, that changed the picture a bit.

A few academics, however, remained very negative about their retirement at the end of the first year. The words of a seventy-year-old professor of preventive medicine revealed his generally unhappy retirement experience:

Awful. I find that, professionally, I'm a displaced person; I have become a nonperson. Subject to nonfatal physical disabilities like asthma. It becomes more of an inconvenience and is the kind of thing that has me being careful about choices. And the usual frailties and disabilities that come along. The problem of rehabilitating a forty-three-year-old marriage. There were so many things that we used to be able to do together and we've grown apart. So that is the sort of situation, because we respond with more enthusiasm than is necessary when I say it's awful. In a remedial way, I am out to build a whole new career for myself. And my wife is less interested in my following her around all morning. I haven't liked anything about retirement; I can't think of anything that I've liked.

Likewise, a home economist, aged sixty-eight, talked about her unhappy first year of retirement:

I have found the first year of retirement to be bad. I had no idea of what I was getting into. And I looked forward to all of the time I would have. Well, I found out that time was terrible; I didn't want to do what I thought I wanted to do. I thought I was going to clean up all the cupboards, and get rid of things, and straighten things out that I hadn't had time to do, and all that. I got bored with that in a very short time. I had trouble putting in those hours. I did have volunteer work at the Old Capitol, which I really felt was not up my alley. It was all right for some people, but I just didn't enjoy taking tourists through the Old Capitol. So the retirement things I planned for really didn't work out that well.

Academics at all other stages of retirement, which ranged up to over thirty years, were asked in the interview, "As far as you are concerned, what do you consider to be the best things about retirement?" I will briefly summarize their responses before turning to the tape-recorded excerpts. Free time to do what you want was mentioned most frequently by retirees from all types of institutions. In fact, availability of free time in retirement was mentioned by at least two-thirds of the retirees from all institutions in both countries. The retired academics used this newly found free time in a wide variety of leisure, volunteer, and service activities, as well as in professional activities. The next most frequently mentioned positive aspect of retirement was freedom from schedules or routine; this was mentioned by about one-third of the retirees from nearly all institutions. Additionally, about one-third of American research university and British university retirees mentioned that they liked having time in retirement to spend on what they enjoyed doing professionally. Only about one-fifth of liberal arts college and comprehensive university retirees, on the other hand, mentioned having free time for professional activities as a positive aspect of retirement. Less frequently mentioned positive aspects of retirement were certain other freedoms: from the pressure or competition, the responsibilities, and the disappointments of work. Interestingly, liberal arts college retirees in the United States identified freedom from the pressure or competition of work far more frequently than did their university counterparts. This may have been a reaction to greater pressure for accountability for students in the liberal arts colleges.

Retirees also discussed the negative aspects of their retirement. More than half of the retired academics across institutions had at least one negative thing to say about retirement. In response to the question "What are the worst things about retirement?" they typically talked about work-related losses. Loss of contact with students and colleagues was most frequently mentioned by retirees from all types of institutions; this loss, however, was mentioned nearly twice as frequently by British academics as by American academics (nearly two-fifths of the former compared to about one-fifth of the latter). One possibility is that the British academics had experienced more one-on-one relationships prior to retirement, particularly with students. Alternatively, British academics may have had fewer opportunities to interact with students and colleagues after retiring than did their American counterparts. Loss of institutional facilities and professional services in retirement was also mentioned more frequently by British than by American academics; in fact, five times as many British academics (25 percent) mentioned loss of facilities and services after retirement as did academics from the comparison American research university (5 percent). Far more American academics, however, identified a common concern of retirees—financial problems—as a negative aspect of retirement than did British academics. The percentage of academics mentioning financial problems varied from 11 to 14 percent for respondents from particular American institutions, whereas for British respondents it was only 2 percent, suggesting that financial security was a greater concern in the United States. Other negative aspects of retirement mentioned by some academics included missing work itself, not enough structure or routine in their lives, not having enough to do, and age-related worries about dependency. Retired academics from the American research university and the British old civic universities were more likely to say that they missed work than were American comprehensive university or liberal arts college retirees; still, this was true for only a small minority of those university retirees (12 percent of research university and 9 percent of old civic university retirees).

The Best Things: Time and Freedom

The overarching themes that pervaded the retirees' positive comments about retirement were time and freedom. Most retired academics talked enthusiastically about the unstructured free time that retirement afforded them and, with it, new possibilities for using that time. This flexibility in time use was mentioned over and over by both retired men and retired women. Thus, a female comprehensive university speech professor, aged seventy-eight, summed up her choices: "I think freedom to either lie in bed and watch the sun rise or get up and do what I please." Her colleague from the same institution, a male pharmacist, aged sixty-eight, put it this way: "You can do what you want when you want to do it." The result was happiness for an eighty-one-year-old male research university professor of education and psychology: "I'm happier than I've ever been in my life. There's something to be said for not having to go to work every morning. I keep pretty busy, but there isn't anything I have to do."

For a British engineer, aged seventy-two, retirement opened up entirely new vistas:

> I think one needs a new lease on life. And so that's then why retirement gives you that. You can also do the things that you are interested in and not for reasons of adding more money or whatever. You tend to get into a groove, as it were. It gives you a chance to change and forces you into activities you didn't realize you were thinking of.

According to this female liberal arts college speech professor, aged seventy-one, more free time made for a more relaxed life:

> One of the best things about retirement is what I'd like to call the "spacious routine" that you have, that things aren't so structured, that your time is your own, and that you can do things pretty much according to your energy and your interests and your abilities. So I expect that maybe the outstanding thing about retirement is the fact that one has the chance for a more relaxed approach to life in general.

Some retirees, like this seventy-three-year-old male British university materials scientist, were pleased to now have more time to spend on a large number of lifetime interests:

> Well, I guess a starting point is that, unlike a lot of people, I've always had an enormous number of interests. I've also been weak-minded enough to get myself on committees, and I commonly found myself chairman of them. So that all through my life I've been much involved in all kinds of activities, most of which have no direct connection with academic work at all. So I can pay more attention and more time to them. Since my earliest recollection,

I've never known a single moment when I've said, "What will I do next?" It was always a question of "Which will I do next?"

A research university home economist, aged seventy-three, also talked about having more time to devote to a number of her interests:

I don't have as many responsibilities as I had before, for one thing, even though I am still very busy. The kind of thing I'm doing isn't as demanding as I did before. I have time to do some things that I wouldn't have had time to do otherwise. I've really taken on a full-time job, but it's only eight to five and I'm used to working every night of the week. It was either a professional meeting or to go back to Macbride Hall. I now have time to do some things and I'm rather deeply involved in church activities. I'm doing some things with professional organizations that I've always been involved in, but I guess I'm still continuing to do some of those things. I'd say that right now is probably one of the nicest times. It's really a very positive time in my life. I feel good; I'm busy; I haven't any problems that I can really think of. And I'd say this is a really nice time in my life. It's a good time. Part of it is that I have plenty to do.

Many retired academics showed much pleasure in finally having the time to read widely on a variety of topics. Two male research university retirees, a seventy-five-year-old professor of Spanish and Portuguese and a seventy-two-year-old professor of speech and dramatic art, commented on their leisure reading:

The norm of classical leisure was to keep active mentally and physically, but not narrowing yourself to a specialty. Keeping alive, as it were, to the broad truths of life. One of the advantages of my retirement is that I have time to read things I never read before.

There is freedom to do some things that you wanted to do but didn't have time to do. I didn't believe I'd ever have time to read some newspapers and magazines. The *Christian Science Monitor*, *Rolling Stone*, *Mineral Digest*. I know nothing about minerals, you might say. I found this interesting.

Others, like this male research university social worker, aged seventy-two, spoke of the advantages of having more family time available in retirement: "There is the opportunity to be at home more. This is an area that I know has hazards. So to speak, get acquainted better with one's partner. To know what goes on at home."

For a considerable number of retired academics, retirement meant something else — having enough time available to do the kind of professional work they enjoyed without being fettered by department meetings, committee work, bureaucratic wranglings, and endless paperwork. Now they could write, paint, compose, and consult, if they so chose. Two male university retirees, a British old civic university psychologist and an American research university psychiatrist, both males aged seventy-five, had very similar things to say about now having time to spend on their own work:

> The freedom to do what you like is the essential thing. You're not committed to all the chores of being a professor. You can spend your whole time on doing what you want to do. That freedom, I think, is the most important. Freedom to work when you like.

> It's a continuation of my own work. I have more variety now. I have in a sense less responsibility. I have more time to do some of the things professionally that I want to do. My income is no worse than it was. I think I have a situation, as a whole, the most satisfying period of my life.

A seventy-two-year-old female home economist and gerontologist from the research university also spoke of the professional activities retirement allowed her time to spend on:

> Well, one of the best things is the opportunity to do the things you wanted to do which you did not have time to do when you were teaching full-time because they may not have been as closely related to your teaching as they would need to be to allow you to take time for them. Things like group affiliations and taking responsibility, like holding office for example, being willing to write things. So I've been asked to write the twelve-year history of the home economics alumni association at my alma mater, and I said I could do it. And it is difficult to take time to do it when you are teaching. Things of that kind.

For some academics, like this research university historian, aged seventy-seven, time spent on his work meant time spent on his main hobby. For him, and for others like him, work was equivalent to play, and it was difficult to separate the two:

Well, I suppose the best thing is that in one sense you are coming to the end of a period of a productive life, and the question that would face you is: Are you now that you are retired going to quit being productive, or not? And while I have been very active, I decided that I wanted to continue the productive side of my life because I got more pleasure, more fun, and more enjoyment out of it and I had so much research already developed, and in the process, one might say in it, that all I could do is — I've got a hobby and it is my big specialty in life. It's as much of a hobby as it is anything else, too. In this sense, I think I am extremely fortunate, because I have been always productive in writing and research since 1928, and the joy to me is that I can continue and that I have a whole vast field that I can carry on in with satisfaction.

Some liberal arts college professors, like these two men, an eighty-eight-year-old professor of Christianity (now department of religion) and an eighty-seven-year-old professor of philosophy, likewise spoke of having more time to spend on professional pursuits. Several decades after retiring, their spirit of inquiry remained steadfast:

I should say the time that you get to do further reading and further work. And I took courses for refreshing my mind both in Greek and in Hebrew and learned my alphabets and my grammar to master the two languages and then I read the history of the church and outlined it in ninety-four typewritten pages. This was material that I had not had time to cover when I was a teacher.

According to my feelings, the best thing was the possibility to do my thinking in the sense of investigation and writing. I was never primarily interested in teaching. Teaching was the only job that could support me in my life. But my main interest was always in thinking and investigation.

Other retired academics spoke of a return to academic roles that had been long abandoned due to their other professional responsibilities. A sixty-nine-year-old research university psychology professor and dean spoke with pleasure of his new options in retirement:

My response to that would be conditioned by the fact that I spent virtually all of my time in administration for the last twenty-nine years. I guess I'd have to say that some of the things I've been reading and working on have always been of interest to me, but I didn't feel at least that I had the time to do it. And so to be able to close the office door and go to the library and not feel guilty about it is another advantage of retirement.

Some retirees, like these two male physicians, one aged sixty-nine and recently retired from the American research university, and the other aged seventy-six and retired for more than a decade from a British old civic university, said they were spending so much time on their professional activities in retirement that they did not consider themselves really retired:

Well, first of all, I'd like my position to be very clear. I am not retired. I have an official retirement within the university with an emeritus status. I am continuing to do precisely the same things that I did while I was active, with the exception that I have no administrative duties. So you're not talking to someone who retired. My habits remain the same, my hours remain the same, so I'm essentially the same as I might have been five years ago. Perhaps in the duties I'm called upon to perform I have a little bit more leeway now than I had before, inasmuch as I'm not beholden, if you will, to an eight-hour working day. I can arrange my schedule to suit my own timing, and I have done so. I've been eliminated from things like university committees, so I can utilize the same time doing things that I'm interested in rather than the perfunctory tasks that are assigned while you're on an active status. And I conceive of that as being about the only change. I am not officially working for the university. I am totally off the university payroll and they have nothing to say about my time.

It's a very hard question to answer because I never retired. I simply changed jobs. Now I'm doing it without pay, but that doesn't bother me. I'm no longer responsible for running the school [tropical medicine]. I'm no longer responsible for the direct treatment of patients. I think those are the two main things. I don't practice medicine at all now. I do things like Medical Boards and research. I'm no longer an active member of the hospital. I never had private practice because I didn't want it. It didn't stop me having to retire in the year in which I turned sixty-five because that's regulated not by the university, but by the government. But there's another line which has kept me actively engaged apart from my work here, and that's my work overseas.

His colleague in pathology, aged eighty-three, also spoke of his work in tropical medicine, a school for which their university was very well known:

I'm practically not retired. I'm retired from the university but I'm not unworking. I went to the School of Tropical Medicine first of all and worked there finishing up some research I've been doing that I enjoyed. That lasted seven years or so. From there, I've carried on in other research.

Satisfaction with the time he was able to devote to professional endeavors was evident in the words of a seventy-six-year-old British physician, retired for a decade, who recounted the variety of his professional involvements since retiring a decade earlier:

When I retired from here as professor of medicine in 1972, but at the same time I became the president of the Royal College of Physicians in London for five years, which meant I had to live mainly in London. It was a big job. I did that from 1972 to 1977. During that time, I met a lot of people in London, and in 1977 I was appointed director of a thing called the Medical Services Study Group, which is a research organization of the Royal College of Physicians. We do medical audit; I call it civilized audit. We do collaborative research and find out why people die. We've published a fair number of papers on the collaborative research. So I do that, and I'm also counselor for the British Heart Foundation; I was chairman of the research section of the British Heart Foundation. I've got a lot of jobs in London. These jobs are honorary jobs. That's the London area. And in this area, I research in genetics and heredity. So I've got an honorary fellowship in the department of genetics. I do quite a lot of work there. I do some research at the zoo in London. I'd say I keep quite busy. I'd say this is the happiest time of my life. So far, the ten years I've had since retirement have been, in a way, the most productive, I would think. Certainly, I've enjoyed it and I am enjoying it very much indeed.

In addition to the advantage of having free time to do whatever they wanted in retirement, the retired academics often talked about enjoying freedom from several aspects of their former work lives. One of these was freedom from the pressures associated with their work, which some found more onerous with advancing age. A seventy-two-year-old musician, a liberal arts college retiree, described her sense of relief from work pressures: "Relief from pressure to keep up. Relief from competition; that's another way of saying the same thing. Particularly the politics; relief from having to contend with politics." A seventy-year-old female physical educator said: "Well, I think you're more relaxed and you're not under pressure. And you're not on a time schedule, which is nice. You feel more free, and you don't have any preparations and something hanging over you all the time." Their male colleague, a sixty-nine-year-old biologist, had some similar feelings: "Well, getting the pressure off. Not having to meet a time schedule; that's the same as getting the pressure off."

University retirees likewise conveyed a sense of relief from job pressures. A female American research university nurse, aged sixty-nine, and a male British old civic university pediatrician, aged sixty-eight, had these comments on the pressures of their jobs:

I guess the best thing is that you don't have to work anymore. After all, all of work isn't that pleasant. There are the difficulties, problems, the harassments which you felt frustrated about. Now you don't have to worry about those frustrating problems.

Certainly one doesn't have the sort of sense of pressure one had when working. There was a sort of feeling that you were working under great stress and tension. That's certainly one thing that is gone. I think that was the first thing to go. There's no longer any set commitments. The opportunities of traveling around which we didn't have before; there was a lack of time before. The opportunity of doing this, not confined to a particular time when you can get off from your place.

Others were happy to be free of the competitive environment associated with their work. According to a seventy-three-year-old research university biochemist, such competitiveness was no longer an important or even an appropriate part of his life:

Well, one's attitudes, of course, have changed greatly. I mean, you are no longer so competitive. A young man, of course, by nature is usually highly competitive, and when one grows older, one just doesn't care anymore. One is not interested in being famous, and doesn't give a damn, and what other people think isn't so important anymore. Well, I'm sure this develops; it doesn't just occur all of a sudden. Gradually, a young man grows older.

A number of retirees also talked with considerable relief about freedom from their work responsibilities. These male research university retirees, a neurologist, aged seventy-two, a psychiatrist, aged seventy-five, and an engineer, aged seventy-six, were all relieved to be free of the administrative duties they relinquished when they retired:

I would think the most important thing is the lack of, or the diminution of, burdensome administrative responsibilities in terms of paperwork, committee meetings, et cetera, which in the aggregate are essentially nonproductive.

I don't have some of the problems I had to deal with as the head of the Child Psychiatry Unit. Because being now a person who goes into two different institutions with a better professional background than most of the people there, I enjoy a little more prestige and respect than I did among colleagues. Perhaps because some of the things I've worked on have come to be a bit better accepted. Because the relations of the people I'm working with are the immediate people, particularly the hospital employees like social workers and psychologists.

I figured my role was to take care of what I called "administrivia." There are millions of things that had to be done. Instead of appointing a committee, I'd just do it. I saw my role as running interference for everybody in the department.

British university retirees also spoke of freedom from administrative duties. An orthopedic surgeon, aged seventy, described his liberation from former responsibilities: "Not having national health service administration committees. I think I was glad not to have so much responsibility—administrative and clinical."

Freedom from other professional responsibilities was also mentioned. His colleague, a historian, aged seventy-four, talked about how retirement had lessened a variety of his burdens:

The absence of routine administrative work and making decisions about student and faculty careers. That's a great burden. Of course, it continues to some extent because you're still writing references for former colleagues or students. It's not enough to be a nuisance, really. It does mean you at least carry on your research or teaching or whatever at your own pace and at your own time.

More frequently mentioned than freedom from job pressures, competition, and responsibilities, however, by retired academics from all institutions in both countries was relief at being no longer constrained by the schedules and routine associated with their jobs. Liberal arts college retirees particularly, like this sixty-eight-year-old male biologist and seventy-eight-year-old female musician, often spoke of freedom from their teaching schedules:

Freedom from the day-to-day responsibilities of being ready for classes, tests, the routines of teaching. That has been a big thing for me, because in the later years I found that quite burdensome. And, for instance, I'd wake up early in the morning and start fretting about the day's work, and I couldn't get back to sleep. And I've gotten over that.

The freedom from a schedule and the constantly ordered schedule that we had in the music department. Every thirty minutes supposedly we would have a new student coming in, and a lot of time we don't immediately bound the class, and some classes I would come back and there was another piano student waiting. And so it was every thirty minutes or every hour supposedly; it couldn't work on that basis, of course. And so I think it's that lack of pressure and freedom of schedule. And I think also the lack of paperwork that comes across the mail every day; that quantity of mail that came into my box every morning, lots of which had to be answered that day or the next day. There were other things you had to look at before you dumped them in the wastebasket, for fear that you missed something that was important. The freedom, I think, to just be me.

A British university retiree, a sixty-eight-year-old male from the faculty of education, also expressed relief at being free of some of the tasks associated with teaching: "Well, I suppose the best thing is not having to get up in the morning and go to work. I'm happy not to cope with the many responsibilities of students' work coming in at several times a year and flooding one. Well, everybody does."

But for most retirees, relief from schedules and routine did not appear to be tied to one particular aspect of the professional role, such as teaching, but was more general. According to an American male research university dental pathologist, aged seventy-two, "The best things about retirement, it seems to me, are the freedom from a rigid schedule and the opportunity to pursue one's former fields of inquiry without interruption." His colleague in periodontics, aged sixty-nine, said that the best thing about retirement for him was "being totally free of deadlines to meet." A geographer from that university, now seventy-seven and living in a retirement community, summed up the thoughts of many of his colleagues:

Well, I have a little more freedom and flexibility in doing the things that I enjoy doing. I'm more free from, oh, administrative and institutional constraints in doing what I want to do. I'm a little bit able to choose what I will do. And, of course, I guess that's attractive to anybody to have freedom of action. And I think that's probably the outstanding thing that I value most in the retirement status.

British academics, like these two male retirees, a seventy-seven-year-old dentist and a sixty-seven-year-old oceanographer, agreed:

The best things of retirement, I would say, are the feelings of freedom to do things in your own time; the tension, the pressure, has gone out. You're not working to the plot all the time. This is particularly noticeable on some of the very bad mornings. You are not obliged to get out and kick the ice off your car. You can sit and read the paper and think, "Oh dear, my colleagues have to get out in all this snow and I'm here having a nice cup of coffee and reading the paper and waiting till the weather improves." When you're not working, you can go out and do things you're interested in. Like gardening and golf. Then we can say, "Oh, we'll go off today; it's a very nice day and we'll go out into the country." We can take a walk.

The best thing is not having to work to a certain timetable. You don't have to be at a place at a certain time, attend meetings on certain dates and times, and so on. There's more flexibility with your time. It's nice not to have things you're responsible to. You're not as responsible if things go wrong. You may take on certain jobs but there's not the same responsibility there.

A completely different, non-work-related aspect of retirement that retired academics talked about when questioned about positive aspects of retirement was retirement migration. Some of the academics who migrated after retirement talked about their move as one of the best things about their retirement. Being able to finally live in a better climate was a real plus about retirement for a sixty-nine-year-old male comprehensive university business professor: "Moving into a warmer climate. Oh, yes, it's something for which we had looked ahead for a long time, planned on. It was a remarkable change from daily routine to a nonstructured routine. And I think that we both thoroughly enjoy our retirement."

A sixty-three-year-old director of health occupations education in the research university transition to retirement study talked about the satisfactions of her retirement move one year after retiring:

> Retirement, for me, is wonderfully satisfying and interesting! My move to Louisville brought me nearer family (my brother and his family) and sharing time with them, neighbors, newfound friends, et cetera, is delightful. I own my own three-bedroom, two-bath house in a lovely subdivision, drive my own Lincoln, am debt free, and am learning my way around the city. I adjusted to this more leisurely life very readily and am extremely happy with my lot.

As noted previously, virtually all of the retired academics discussed at least one positive aspect of their retirement; no more than 3 percent of retirees from either the United States or the United Kingdom said there were no positive aspects at all about retirement. Those academics who said there was nothing positive about retirement, however, usually said so in strong terms. The words of this seventy-one-year-old male British university radiologist convey the feelings of those who had nothing good to say about retirement:

> I don't [think there are any positive aspects]. I don't like retirement. I don't like retiring, because assuming I was still fit, there's no hell of a reason why I couldn't go on doing my job. And I still keep up with all my professional journals, and I thank God that they usually have cheaper subscriptions for retired gents, and I still keep up membership in my professional bodies. And I still get a certain amount of requests for advice and I get an occasional book to review. But that's not easy, because these days, teaching in radiology, things are changing so fast with imaging technology, that one gets left behind. I enjoyed my work and I didn't particularly want to give it up.

The Worst Thing: Loss of the Professional Role

Although most of the academics who identified losses in retirement talked of loss of their students, colleagues, facilities, and work itself, a few said they felt that they no longer belonged to their institution, that they felt cut off from it. What was being communicated was a feeling of loss not just of the professional role, but of professional identity. An eighty-one-year-old British female academic specializing in Hispanic studies talked of retirement as "being on the scrap heap." A seventy-eight-year-old American research university biochemist expressed his feelings similarly: "The worst thing about retirement is the feeling that you no longer belong. You are left high and dry; you can't continue as you did before." Other retirees, including two male American research university physicians, aged seventy-two and seventy, and a male British chemist, aged ninety-one, elaborated on these feelings of loss:

> The devastating emotional effects of forced retirement, not the financial; the business of being out of it. I think if one were doing piecework or putting nuts or bolts on an automobile, you would look forward to retirement. But if you've been a professional person all your life, it's an entirely different thing. It's something you don't like to part with quickly and abruptly.

> I think at times, infrequently, I become paranoid. That I'm an old horse out to pasture who just doesn't know anything. But that's very infrequent. All that has to happen is a problem case come up, then what do you think? Then there I am right back. And also the idea that you're finished. You're finished. No one ever promised me a bed of roses. There is a fact about retirement that says you're cut off from the institution. Well, I got moved into this office which has absolutely no windows. Even a prison cell has windows. Being the sensitive person that I am, I respond to this closed-in feeling. The way I took care of that psychologically is that I've never seen a museum with windows in it. So I'm going to change this office space into a little museum and I'm still working on that. It is one aspect of my particular pattern of retirement that I was asked to change my office. Everything you're used to, suddenly cut off from it.

> The worst thing in retirement is the tendency to feel that the struggle is over, I'm finished with it, why should I bother myself with anything. This, in my mind, is a fatal attitude because one

lives by activity and if you deliberately disrupt that activity you lay yourself open to decay. Both physical and mental.

Loss of professional status and influence after retiring was evident in the comments of a seventy-year-old male British orthopedic surgeon, who talked about loss of power:

> It is a very curious thing, because I wouldn't have said I was a very power-loving person, but the fact is that once you retire nobody wants to take your decision on anything or ask you a question. One minute everyone is asking you, waiting for you to do things; the next minute you are a nobody.

A few retirees were openly angry at their institutions for forgetting them, like this eighty-two-year-old female professor of secretarial science from the American comprehensive university:

> I think the worst things are a feeling of separation, of neglect. All of a sudden, you are not part of the ongoing. For instance, I have felt very much as one who was just dropped. There are some ways in which I have had a few very good friends, two particularly, who have kept me in touch, and we have been able to get a foursome that we play bridge together quite frequently. But that doesn't involve me in the life of the institution. I have never been invited back to a faculty meeting. Never have been invited or notified of even the ceremonial times, or things like that. Some institutions are better doing that. I feel that this is one of the things where the university is very thoughtless. In the past, I knew certain faculty members who continued to come back to commencement and take part in the faculty procession and that sort of thing. I think it's thoughtlessness, thoughtlessness on the part of the people who haven't experienced this. I don't suppose they can.

The most common loss described by these academics, however, was loss of contact with their students and colleagues. The retirees mentioned missing students more frequently than missing colleagues, and their comments pointing to loss of their students were among the most poignant in the interview. An eighty-three-year-old liberal arts college musician, now living in a retirement facility and having to adjust to what she called "old people," said simply: "I miss working with young people." Another liberal arts college retiree, a seventy-year-old male Spanish professor, agreed:

> I miss my students. I still have contact with my colleagues a lot. I still work for the college part-time as director of summer school in Spain, so I have contact with my colleagues in the department and in other departments, but I miss the opportunity of teaching and meeting with the students especially. If you're not teaching, you don't see your students. You don't have the opportunity to meet with them and talk with them and even socialize.

The central importance of teaching for liberal arts college professors was noted by a seventy-four-year-old political science professor and a seventy-two-year-old English professor, both males:

> I miss the contact with young minds. I very definitely miss that. To engage the imagination in nonstereotyped directions. I think my mind was strong in its ability to explicate texts and thereby engage the imagination of outstanding students, and at the same time not bore the less intelligent students.

> I miss teaching because I enjoyed it. I enjoyed the contact with the students. Basically, I enjoyed my work. The only thing I didn't like was grading papers and a few things like that. I have done some research and publication, but I'm not basically a research man. You can't be at a small college. But that didn't bother me.

Although there was relatively less emphasis on time spent in teaching at most of the universities than at the liberal arts colleges, retirees from the universities also spoke of missing teaching and their students. After many years of retirement, an American research university historian, aged eighty-four, could still say: "I miss my students more than anything I can imagine. I really enjoyed my classes very much. I turned out some very nice people." His colleagues, a seventy-three-year-old male speech and dramatic art professor and a sixty-nine-year-old female nursing professor, likewise talked about what they missed about their students:

I miss observing the intellectual and scholarly development of students. Their enlarging capacity, if they do enlarge. Their capacity to comprehend and think about and speak and write about things that matter in the areas of experience and thought we were involved in.

I miss the contact with the young students, the young viewpoint. I have a kind of dread of getting narrow-minded, or not understanding or knowing. I'd kind of like to know what they are thinking. I even enjoy just getting on the Cambus [the campus bus system] and just riding around on it. Young people are very friendly these days, you know, they really are.

A British old civic university architect, aged seventy-six, and his colleague in education, aged sixty-nine, expressed similar sentiments:

Well, one misses the contact with students, which is something I have always enormously enjoyed. I do miss the enjoyment that I had in teaching. What I've always been interested in too, while I was still teaching at the university, was getting architecture across to the public. And that means that I do need to some extent to continue some teaching and occasionally giving lectures to a public audience. And so that at least retains a little.

I miss the students very much. The lack of intellectual stimulus which you get from your students. And from your colleagues, of course. But you don't get so much intellectual stimulation from your colleagues. You always do with your students. Teaching I always enjoyed. So far as the feedback I could get from the students, and colleagues to some extent, I think I must have been fairly successful because the students seemed to enjoy the relations we had, and they kept coming back to me afterwards.

The love of teaching and devotion to students that characterized many of the retired academics was summed up by a seventy-eight-year-old male economist from the research university, who found teaching to be his major source of satisfaction:

I leave no reputation as a profound scholar and as a great publisher, but I think I leave a reputation as a good classroom teacher.

As the years went by, I found myself spending more time on preparing for class discussion. I would say to myself after even twenty to twenty-five years of teaching, "This is the thing I enjoy."

A central aspect of the teaching role identified by retired academics from both the British old civic and American research universities was the training and mentoring of graduate students, many of whom would become the next generation of academics. The voices of a British sixty-eight-year-old electrical engineer and of two academics from the American research university, an English professor, aged sixty-nine, and a zoologist, aged seventy-four, all males, conveyed the importance of graduate students in their lives:

> Without any question, it's the lack of company of people who were working on the same kind of thing that I was working on and whom I saw day to day, at some times over many years, and of whom there were quite a number of young chaps who were students of mine, particularly Ph.D. students, and who had grown up and become colleagues. Their company was very precious to me and I miss it.

> Yes, the closeness to graduate students. It's a kind of parental relationship, so that cutting that off makes a significant difference. You become friends. I take this seriously and for a long time have had close contacts with students, endeavoring to help them along. It is one of the most rewarding parts of teaching. I find dissertation work one of the most rewarding forms of teaching. You don't just read it and okay it, but discuss things with the student. However bright the student, the dissertation can be improved.

> Well, I don't have the contact with students. I think this would be the most important. Although many of the students come over and visit me and ask for advice. I had — I think when I retired, the students had a little party for me. And later on, I had fifty-some Ph.D.s that were back as well as a number of master's students. It's something lasting.

Retired academics also missed their colleagues, not only because they provided professional stimulation and collegiality, but because of the social interaction associated with the workplace across occupations. As a seventy-two-year-old female musician from a liberal arts college put it: "Of course I miss the social contacts with my peers, my colleagues." A seventy-nine-year-old male research university mathematician, who was in poor health, said sadly: "There is the matter of isolation from your colleagues. Most of them do not come to call." And a newly retired seventy-one-year-old photography professor from the same university spoke of his loss of contact with colleagues: "I suppose, having been a very gregarious person, I found it a little bit disturbing not being able to have as much contact with all the people in my department." Retirement could also raise the risk of growing apart intellectually from former colleagues and friends over time, as was noted by the oldest British respondent, a ninety-one-year-old chemist (this man, incidentally, had taught at another institution after his retirement until he was eighty-four years of age): "I think the worst feature of retirement is the risk of losing the friends, many friends who have similar interests to you whilst you were active and may have not kept up with those interests in their retirement. And colleagues, mostly."

Even when collegial relationships had been less than ideal, the retirees missed the personal associations of their college or university. A comprehensive university historian, aged seventy, described his departmental experience:

> Well, I think the principal thing probably would be contact with my colleagues. Although there, even when I was in the department, we had plenty of contacts certainly, but the contact was almost always about nuts and bolts. About, well, you know, the departmental questions; you have a departmental meeting; all right, it's about some kind of departmental business. But even when I was there I had the feeling that we never really had much opportunity or took the time to get together and talk about history. It was always — people were always dealing with some kinds of problem: some question of policy, some question of programs, or some memo that the dean wants. So that even when I was there I felt that one of our lacks was that we just never seemed to take the time and talk about history. Well, I miss that, although I'm qualifying it,

saying you never really had it to a great extent when I was there, and I don't believe many departments do.

Something else that could be difficult to deal with was the realization that departments and colleagues could get along without you, as was the case for this seventy-one-year-old medical pathologist in the transition to retirement study (the following comments are from his postretirement interview one year after retirement):

> I think as you approach retirement you begin to feel gradually cut off from some things, even though you're still involved in them and still feel competent doing these things. There is a feeling that perhaps it isn't very important because you're going to stop doing them pretty soon. There are other people waiting to take over. So there is a certain amount of that feeling. You have sort of a feeling of diminished importance. I noticed that particularly since I don't think I would feel as needed anyway, because we have more people, we're better staffed than we were. Consequently, they can get along without me better than they could a couple of years ago.

Somewhat surprising was that relatively few of the retired academics mentioned missing work itself as being a negative aspect of retirement. One possible reason for this was that the majority of academics who wished to do so had found opportunities to continue at least some aspects of their professional work in retirement, while not being burdened by the duties that many found onerous during their preretirement careers. Some academics took strong positions on work and retirement. A seventy-year-old research university classics professor said: "If you enjoyed your work, then you don't enjoy your retirement unless you continue in some way." Her colleague from physical education, aged seventy-two, expressed her opinion even more forcefully: "If they don't enjoy their work, they are tickled to death to retire. If they did enjoy it, retirement is an insult."

Nostalgia for general involvement in professional work was expressed by a British university mathematician, aged sixty-six, who cited government cutbacks in the universities as a factor in his recent retirement decision: "It's a situation where one was on a lot of faculty and department and university committees and felt that you were involved in what was going on. And suddenly that's all, and you're talking about your years at the university over the coffee table."

Another recently retired academic, a sixty-five-year-old nurse in the transition to retirement study, said that she would "be like a horse going to the barn. I won't be around when school starts next fall. Hard not to come back when school starts."

A few academics expressed an utterly bleak view of their loss of the work role. An eighty-four-year-old male research university historian felt this way even after sixteen years of retirement:

> I have to endure this business of being a retired professor. There were hundreds of people who just had my course, you see. I think it would be nice to send us all to an undertaker when we retire. I think we have had our life; there's nothing ahead of us, you see, that you plan on or that you can be ambitious about. I used to think I'd do a lot of things that I didn't do, and if I had lived long enough I probably would have done some of them. I wanted to be a professor, and I didn't want to be anything else. And I've enjoyed being a professor more than any human being could enjoy anything. I've been lucky in that respect.

Only a small number of American academics mentioned loss of facilities and professional services as one of the negative things about retirement. Far more British than American academics, however, mentioned this loss, probably because fewer British retirees had such facilities as office space, secretarial assistance, and laboratories available. The British retirees frequently expressed concerns, in particular, about lack of secretarial help. A seventy-year-old botanist said that "the biggest problem is lack of a secretary. You have to do it yourself. It consumes time." His colleague, a seventy-one-year-old engineer, also lamented his lack of secretarial help: "I haven't got a secretary anymore and I can't type. So my letters get much shorter than they were." A seventy-year-old dentist said that for him "the major thing is not having a secretary. I'm handicapped by the fact that I can barely read my own handwriting." And a pathologist, aged eighty-three, talked about how he had handled the lack of secretarial help and then offered direction for his university: "Before I retired, I had a secretary. When I retired, for a couple of years I was able to pay for a secretary.

The last few years or so I have had no secretary. I'm strongly under the opinion that retirees should be provided with a secretary."

Another British retiree, a seventy-three-year-old civil engineer, spoke of his lack of workshop space: "Yes, one hasn't gotten the access to workshop facilities which the engineering side has. The free access that one had."

Lack of office space could be an issue for both British and American academics. A comprehensive university astronomer, aged seventy-four, recounted his experience in having to move from his office:

> My one really strenuous and quite traumatic experience was the clean-out of my office. If the university had not allowed me several weeks, I could not have made it. One should be aware of this problem well ahead of time and get started several weeks in advance. Files: these will almost certainly contain much superfluous material and need culling and some reorganization unless one has had a great deal of very competent secretarial assistance. Of course, the fact that I was a one-man department had much to do with my difficulties, combined with the fact that I never had full-time or professional secretaries except while directing institutes. Library: again, get started well in advance. Unless one has plenty of shelf room at home, a drastic and sometimes almost heart-breaking culling out is necessary. Some books I was able to contribute to the departmental or university library. I had a "free — help yourself" shelf set up outside my office door. Finally, I boxed the remainder of those I had no room for at home and took them to Planned Parenthood for their annual book sale, but how many communities have that outlet? Incidentally, that gives a chance for an income tax deduction. My move-out took two weeks and left me so exhausted that I had to go off to the woods and lake and hermit-it for five days. More advance planning and an earlier start might have eased the ordeal a lot.

For academics who had left their preretirement community after retiring, irrespective of institution or nation, the loss of facilities and services could be a particular problem. Library privileges, for instance, were generally available to retirees who continued to live in their preretirement communities, but adequate libraries might not be available for those who migrated after retiring. An American research university professor of counselor education, aged seventy-four, talked about the facilities he no longer had: "The resources of the library is something I miss. And I miss terribly the clerical help. I think we tend to undervalue how important a good secretary who can also maintain your files can be."

In addition to work-related losses, the retired academics talked about several other concerns as negative aspects of retirement. These included not having enough structure or routine in their lives, financial problems, and worries about dependency. Such concerns are hardly unique to retired academics and are shared by retirees from all walks of life. It is interesting to note that the academics saw the lack of structure or routine in retirement as both positive and negative. For some, a less-structured existence was perceived as an advantage, whereas for others it was a disadvantage, illustrating how differently people can react to the same phenomenon. Concerns about lack of structure and loss of the academic routine were expressed by this newly retired research university professor of family practice, aged seventy, one year after his retirement:

> The certain anxiety I get sometimes when I think I ought to be working. Amazingly, it's in the evening when I've not done anything much all day, and I feel like I have to do something. I'm coming to the office Monday, Tuesday, and Wednesday, and working on my research. It's this feeling that I'm retired Thursday, Friday, Saturday, and Sunday. It's really Thursday and Friday and maybe Saturday that I have a feeling that I ought to be doing something. What was I going to do today? I guess I'm used to structure. I'm used to having my day mapped out for me and it isn't anymore.

A British old civic university engineer, aged seventy-one, and an American research university art historian, aged seventy, both males who had been retired for several years, also spoke of the need to establish a new structure for their days:

The sudden realization, which I really hadn't expected, of some cessation of the necessity of having to get up in the morning and go to work. And that was a surprise. The feeling, the realization, that it didn't really matter if I got up or not. That was the sort of feeling I had. The truth is, I get up an hour earlier than I ever did before. Oh, yes, I've still got lots of things to do, and most days I'm doing something; it's just this getting in here at nine o'clock on the days I was here. Just the timing, dictated by outside circumstances.

A disciplined day also has its advantages. I have to establish a whole new world in which I make my own discipline. One would think that having so much time would be wonderful. I have been blocked by not establishing discipline.

Financial concerns about retirement, a major issue for many retired people, were mentioned by a relatively small minority of American academics and by only a few British academics. Undoubtedly, improved pension and Social Security benefits in the 1970s and 1980s played a role in this majority assessment of financial adequacy. The general economic impact of retirement on people, however, was summed up by a seventy-eight-year-old female musician: "Well, of course you miss the salary. You can't help missing that check coming in. Unless you're fortunate enough to have arranged so that you have something to compensate for it." A seventy-four-year-old male political scientist said: "I suppose considering the economic conditions of the country and the world, you have to have some concern about money. Particularly the fear of inflation eroding what you have."

Some of the retirees spoke of the financial picture of retired academics in general and not necessarily of their own financial situation. A few maintained that the overall financial picture of retired academics was poor. According to a seventy-four-year-old research university chemical engineer, "Most of the retirees do not really have an adequate retirement income." His colleagues, a biochemist and anatomist, both males aged seventy-three, offered more details on what they believed to be the general financial picture:

Many university professors are just in a jam. I would suspect that some men, let's say in English or history or some of the humanities, they may be having trouble. We in the sciences are somewhat better off. For instance, we are paid twelve-month benefits. Some of these fellows haven't been able to get summer teaching. Some don't have much savings to speak of. I would suspect there are some cases of hardship.

Many people do have problems in retirement because they may have financial problems which may be very discouraging and very serious to them. Particularly here, the institution of TIAA/CREF was very late. So the older people are not doing as well as the younger people.

A recently retired professor of rhetoric and English, aged sixty-five, from the research university said that his own situation would have been difficult had he not had income from other sources:

Well, a thing that would have made me unhappy, I think, would have been the salary and the retirement benefits if I hadn't had Air Force retirement all along. I frankly don't know how some of my colleagues are going to manage on the retirement that they will have. It's going to be a really major change in their standard of living. I don't know what can be done about it. In some way people should be assisted or directed or forced to prepare for a happy retirement by having better income after retirement.

The most common financial concern expressed by the retired academics was fear of inflation and of their money running out in the future, rather than concern for existing financial problems. The words of a sixty-seven-year-old research university nurse epitomized concerns about outliving one's income:

I think the uncertainty of the finances is the worst thing. You keep hearing all the time of inflation. And you know about it. And you know you are now on a fixed income. And you wonder, you know, will your money hold out your life? And will you be able to be an independent individual? My mother died in 1972 when she was ninety-two. My father died in 1966 when he was ninety-six.

What these retirees wanted was long-term financial independence. A seventy-four-year-old male liberal arts college English professor summed up this general desire: "Well, I mentioned the financial thing. If you are not more or less secure financially, retirement can be much more of a shock and traumatic. I think we've always prized our independence, and, of course, without financial independence, you don't have any independence, really."

Some of the retired academics also spoke of their concerns about eventual physical decline and dependency in later life. The issue of dependency was brought to the forefront for some by the milestone of retirement, which signaled to them the beginning of old age. Thus, a seventy-three-year-old British mechanical engineer said he thought the worst thing about retirement was "getting older." Likewise, a seventy-one-year-old astronomer from the American research university said that what he liked least about retirement was "the heightened realization that I am getting old and have relatively few years to do the many things that I like to do." His colleague, a biochemist aged seventy-three, elaborated on the themes of aging and dependency:

> As a man grows older, the effects of age begin to show. Some minor or major medical problems begin to appear. They hamper your mobility and in terms of the things that you can do. I think that's the worst thing that happens — deterioration of the old. And that's inevitable. And sometimes it's worse for the other people. I think one of the things that frighten an old person, as Charles de Gaulle would say, "Yes, there is one thing I am afraid of; that when I grow old, I will become dependent and will be unable to take care of myself." He said that was the only thing he was ever afraid of. That's true of a number of us. That we are afraid that the time will come that we will be dependent. You get to a physical state that you simply cannot cope. There are a number of people who are unlucky enough to live too long. There are people who know when to die. Some people know how to die with elegance. Other people just drag it out, don't ever know when to die.

A research university professor of communication studies, aged sixty-five and scheduled to retire within a few months, offered his solution to this: "The whole idea of declining and being useless is an awful thought. I've thought about dying in class with my boots on."

For those retirees who had already developed serious health problems, dependency was a current concern and had become an important issue in their lives. A nearly blind eighty-six-year-old male liberal arts college professor of economics and business administration said: "There is the natural decay that age imposes; in my case, loss of eyesight. I don't like to be dependent." One of the oldest British retirees, a ninety-year-old pharmacist suffering from multiple health conditions—a heart condition, cataracts, and thyroid problems—spoke of his past and his present: "I have enjoyed my life, but I don't enjoy my life now, with all my handicaps."

It was not only the very old retirees who suffered these health problems and consequently were forced to modify their lifestyles. Two men who were still in their sixties, a liberal arts college speech professor, aged sixty-eight, and a comprehensive university historian, aged sixty-nine, talked about what had happened to them:

> I suppose that's one of the things that has offered me problems, personally, the fact that I've had to fight the health problem. And that has colored my evaluation of every day, practically. If I could find the answer to feeling better, life would take on a new luster and a new adventure, and we probably would be interested in doing some travel, or some other involvements that would be exciting. But when you're not feeling well, then, obviously, you do the best you can with each day that comes, and you feel you're almost better off being right at home. That's pretty much a definite part of what I've had to face for the last couple of years.

> Health problems which you have anyway, I suppose. In my particular case, I've had a series of eye operations. I've always had eye problems, and it's something you can't get rid of. That has been the main problem. And that of course has generated other problems. I think the principal problem is the health problems.

A final response elicited by the question "What are the worst things about retirement?" deserves mention. That response had to do with the ageism that is prevalent in our society: negative attitudes toward older people that are held and expressed by younger people. A British psychologist, aged seventy-four, connected such ageism to her retirement:

I don't find that retirement itself is the negative thing. The negative thing is the aging. This is real important. The other thing is the social aspect of it. It is other people's attitudes to retirement. When I make an excuse and say I can't do something, I can't come to tea, because I've got this to do, they say, "I thought you were retired." As if they think I'm going to sit down and do nothing. And I'm not going to sit and do nothing. It's other people's attitudes and what they think retirement is.

Voices of Experience: Suggestions for Those Who Are Soon to Retire

At the beginning of the interview, retirees were told that we believed that people who were about to retire might better anticipate both the problems and satisfactions of retirement if they could learn from persons like themselves who were already retired and that we would therefore appreciate their advice to present and future retirees based on their own experiences. The question that was asked to tap their advice to future retirees was "What are some suggestions you would make for those who are soon to retire?" The retired academics most frequently answered that people should stay active in retirement and that they should plan ahead for their retirement. Academics from the British old civic universities were less likely to mention the importance of planning ahead (29 percent) than were their American research university counterparts (46 percent). As we saw earlier, British academics had actually engaged in significantly less retirement planning, particularly financial planning, than had their American counterparts, so it is not unreasonable that they would not emphasize retirement planning for others. The advice about planning that was offered by a sixty-nine-year-old engineer who participated in the American research university transition to retirement study was typical of many of his colleagues:

I can [offer advice] out of my own experience, although I'm certain to sound presumptuous in doing it. I think one should study and plan for his retirement. Not have any surprises. You better know what life is going to be like. Now many people take a lot of care about their financial situation and they should, but they seem to think that's all, or if not all at least the most important. I don't think it is. We can all live with whatever amount of money we're going to get. But if we don't have some way of controlling our lives and continuing to enjoy them, we're going to be in real trouble. I say that because I've seen people who have not and have been in real trouble.

A male liberal arts college philosopher, aged eighty-seven, urged people to not put off thinking about their retirement so as to be adequately prepared for it when it actually occurred:

I would say that if they hadn't thought already of this, it would be necessary for them to think about retirement and to be prepared for it. Because this radical turning in life is very strong. But I was always waiting for my retirement; therefore, I didn't experience it as a catastrophe. It was only a change for the first year in the sense that my secondary interest was in teaching. I did not teach anymore for about four years or so. But this was somehow significant for me. For those who don't have such an attitude, it would be extremely important for them to think about it; otherwise, they can have troubles. Psychological troubles.

Other academics, like this sixty-seven-year-old liberal arts college professor of education and sixty-five-year-old research university professor of engineering, both males, suggested that people should plan for retirement well ahead of the actual event:

I would suggest starting early. Now I started my own at about age sixty. I suppose one could start earlier than that, certainly. Be thinking about it for a long ways ahead and think about all the options and possibilities about it and then to make up one's mind about it. I think that's perhaps one of the more difficult things. Some people I know anyway just can't retire, but I think one must get oneself in a frame of mind saying, "Well, look at age sixty-five or at whatever age one chooses; this is it, and I'm going to live with it." A mental set is a good way to put it. I'm talking about planning and this includes financial, religious, psychological, and everything else.

Start planning for it ten years in advance, which I did. Be sure that they have something they plan to do after they retire. Because if they just plan on sitting in the rocking chair on the front porch, that's deadly. I don't believe you can start planning too early on it. Start thinking about it. You don't have to write down anything definite, but at least start thinking about it. I believe it was, oh, five or six years ago, when I went to that retirement seminar. Maybe ten years is a little bit early to start planning. At least they can start thinking about it from time to time. I'm sure I started thinking about it at least ten years ago. And I wrote to some places for articles on retirement. I subscribed to the AARP [American Association of Retired Persons] magazine, *Modern Maturity*, several years ago and got information from AIM [Association for Independent Maturity] and found those helpful. My own experience is that a person should think ahead on it. Well, for two reasons. Planning ahead doesn't hurt a bit, but if you don't, it'd seem to be quite a traumatic experience to be working one day knowing that you can't go back the next, without any thought prior to that point. If you plan ahead, the emotional shock is, as far as I'm concerned, eliminated. Of course, this would vary with the individual too.

The retirees also urged future retirees to plan ahead for specific aspects of their retirement such as time use, finances, and where to live. A sixty-nine-year-old British male university dentist suggested that preretirees plan ahead for how they would use their time in retirement: "Oh, yes. When you retire, you shouldn't just waste your time, but plan for the years ahead. You should think, 'How can I best use my time to the benefit of mankind?'" A seventy-one-year-old male American research university musician said: "Well, I think you should begin planning on how you're going to spend your time so you don't become frantic at the last minute. You're irritable because you have nothing to do. It would become a gradual adjustment to change from a very busy schedule to one that is full of leisure."

Financial planning was also strongly recommended by the retirees. Sometimes this advice was based on hindsight, as with this male liberal arts college English professor, aged seventy-two: "I know certain mistakes I made. I think I would advise anyone to be more careful with their money than I was." A sixty-eight-year-old male physiologist from the United Kingdom agreed with him: "You've got to think about your financial needs and your financial situation." An American comprehensive university astronomer, aged seventy-four, outlined specific actions that he believed would help in financial planning: "I think the obvious thing, such as do the best you can to accumulate sufficient savings, plan what you're going to do about your retirement income, how you're going to take it. As the time approaches, watch what the stock market is doing and what interest rates are doing."

A final suggestion for retirement planning offered by the retired academics was to carefully consider where one wished to live in retirement. A comprehensive university social scientist, aged seventy-one, who had migrated after retiring, gave his thoughts on this: "Plan your retirement, where you want to retire. And be sure you get a satisfactory place which you would like to retire in." However, the need to exercise caution about moving was expressed by a sixty-seven-year-old female English professor from one of the liberal arts colleges: "I would say before you sell your house and move to another community, consider carefully what you're doing. How many friends you would have in the other community. I would certainly advise to try it on a trial basis before I would make the commitment. Cutting yourself off from your home base could be, well, I would think twice about giving up your home."

Along with planning for retirement, staying active in retirement was the other major piece of advice given by large numbers of academic retirees from all institutions and in both countries. The comments of a female liberal arts college musician, aged seventy-eight, and a male research university ophthalmologist, aged seventy-three, reflected their conviction that staying active after retiring was central to a satisfying life:

> I think everybody that retires must have something to do to keep them busy. I can think of nothing worse than having nothing to do. I have a friend who is a little older than I, who on her retirement didn't have enough funds and anyplace to go. She's in a nursing home, and when I visit her I feel that she is just sitting and

waiting for time to pass. I'm far from this because there isn't nearly enough time in my retirement. I would say they must have had something. I'm not sure it's a hobby, it must be some goal; something that will make life worth living for them when they do retire.

I think many people hate the process of retiring, the uncertainty of what they're going to be doing. But actually, once they're retired and find their niche, where they belong in society, and don't feel like a useless fifth wheel, once you get over that, I think that you can really enjoy retirement.

Some retirees, like this seventy-four-year-old male comprehensive university astronomer, felt that new activities should be undertaken before one actually retires in order to help facilitate the retirement transition:

I would urge anyone whose whole activity and interest has been the job — unlikely with faculty people, but not unknown — to be sure to start a few years ahead to awaken all sorts of interests that may have been dormant — in all kinds of activities, intellectual and arts interests, also athletic participation, and start, so much as time can be found, to activate these interests and to have gotten a start in pursuing them when retirement time arrives. This will greatly ease the shock of sudden time to kill. Included is travel, which will be vastly more interesting if such things as local and foreign cultures, history, arts, and architecture are learned. A semi-retired period would facilitate this.

Two male British university retirees in their mid-seventies, one in education and the other in pediatrics, agreed that retirement was a time to add new activities to one's repertoire:

Well, I think from my own experience, I would suggest expanding your interests or changing your interests. And keeping up with academic work of some sort. I mean some people can write in their retirement, others travel, and many people do what I did, that is, attend extramural classes in whatever subject interests you. I think it's very stimulating. That's one of my criticisms of academic people is brain curd. I think a change of interest or a change of subject or even a change of entertainment, things of that sort are good. It's very challenging because another problem I would say of retirement is the lack of challenge. The lack of having to get yourself to a certain place every time every morning. A lot of the challenges go, and therefore I would think to create new ones is a good thing.

Not to hesitate to start activities which they don't happen to have taken part in before, because they are new. Because they may find that they are surprisingly satisfying.

And an American research university professor of French and secondary education, aged seventy-two, cautioned against being limited in later life by one's academic specialization: "The importance of remaining active as the years advance. It need not be in the fields of specialization of one's academic life. In fact, better not! For some, as it was at first for us, it was travel. For others of my past colleagues it has been gardening, golf, community service, or the pursuit of a hobby."

Whether the activities were new or not, the retirees agreed that whatever one chose to do in retirement should be of deep interest and should make a contribution. The importance of personally meaningful and productive activity after retiring was addressed by an active seventy-one-year-old female professor of art history and classics, also from the research university:

That would be my primary one, that you either have something you've been working on and want to continue to work on or you have a hobby. Not just something that fills up time, but something that really interests you, that you want to work on, you want to do. In a way it helps structure your time because you can lose hours, days, by just doing nothing. I think you have to do something so you don't feel that there are empty periods in your day that you don't know what to do with. And also to keep up contacts with your colleagues and with some of your students if you can. Activities are another way to get involved. The elderly volunteer services of some sort. To feel like you do have contact with the outside world and that you are perhaps contributing.

The idea of not wasting the time that remained to him was also on the mind of a liberal arts college biologist, aged sixty-nine: "People postpone doing certain things too long and in some cases health fails or something else happens and they cannot do them. If people have a certain dream, I would urge that they do it, not put it off too long."

In addition to their recommendations for staying active and planning ahead, retired academics suggested that others who were soon to retire should continue their work in retirement. British academics were considerably more likely (32 percent) than their American research university counterparts to suggest continuation of academic work (11 percent). The following comments from retired academics from the two British universities are illustrative. All of the responses are from men in their early to mid-seventies; however, the disciplines they represent are varied: modern history, botany, and education.

> I think the best thing an academic can do when he retires is going on being an academic. I know of persons who haven't done much research and then retirement leaves a gap. Usually they are people who prided themselves on teaching rather than contributing to knowledge. For them, I would suggest that they take up something completely different and retrain for something else, unless they have an interest in gardening or sports or something else like that. One of the things I think is important in a way is that some academics when they retire, they dispose of their books. It's a reason to suggest that retired people, if they are still interested in their subject, that they continue to retain their books and papers because they are a necessary part of their continued work.

> I think the thing to do is to develop some new line of work which you can follow up with when you leave. If you can, keep some friends and colleagues to have some collaboration with. Most people have some special interests, which allows them to carry on with some colleagues.

> Perhaps work a little bit even after you've retired, if you can. This does two things. One, it preserves to some extent your sense of status not in any sense of social importance, but in the sense of self-identity importance. It's a psychological matter, that one is re-

garded by others in a certain way, often in quite different ways by different people, but they help to build up and reinforce one's impression of one's self. You can feel in a total vacuum and I think many people who retire do so when they suddenly drop out of a pattern.

American academics, particularly university retirees, also spoke of the importance of continuing one's life work in retirement. Suggestions were offered by a recently retired research university political scientist, aged seventy-one, who spoke from the experience of his first year of retirement:

The most interesting and satisfying experience of the year was a trip to South Africa. The political science association there invited me down at their expense to give a keynote address at their national conference, providing I spend a month there traveling around and learning about South Africa, also at their expense. I spent two and one-half months preparing that address. I have spent four months out of the last twelve devoted to that. I spent the last two months revising a book manuscript, so I have it done now. I feel that I am in a fortunate position here because for many years I've enjoyed research and writing, and I've been able to do that more fully since retiring than I could before. So anybody who has the interest and the aptitude for research and writing ought to cultivate that talent so as to be able to pursue it in retirement. It's always important to feel that you have something to do that's worthwhile, and I could suppose that a person who retired and then, simply without anything to do that he regarded as worthwhile, I would expect such a person to be very unhappy.

His colleague, a seventy-eight-year-old male pharmacist who had been retired for a much longer period, suggested other routes for staying professionally active in retirement:

I would suggest that they retire earlier from administrative responsibilities and allow themselves to get back into their own field. I stayed in the administrative end far too long. I would suggest that they think about retiring earlier than sixty-eight. There are many opportunities for people. I had opportunities after I retired to go teach in foreign countries and lecture in foreign countries, and those would be the things that I would think the people would like to do.

And one of the oldest research university retirees, a ninety-six-year-old English professor who lived in a nursing home because of his physical infirmities, offered this piece of advice to people who were not yet retired: "The sacredness to have a goal later in life. The whole thing of art for art's sake."

Retired academics also suggested to preretirees that they either keep in touch with former students and colleagues or make new contacts related to their profession during retirement. The importance of such contacts, related either directly or indirectly to one's former work role, was noted by two female academics, a British old civic university retiree, aged seventy-eight, from the faculty of education and an American research university retiree, aged seventy-six, from the institute for child development:

> If you can get into things where you are connected with other people, I think that is a good thing also. For instance, I'm the president of the historical association and it is run by my old students. I don't do much for it but they come to me and we discuss it. I'm also taking a more active part in the local liberal associations. I'm on various committees. I meet a lot of people that way. So I'm very busy, busy as I can handle.

> I kept up contacts with a variety of people and with a program that was very much related to my work, both university and town. So that my contacts changed to some extent, but it keeps me in enough contact so that I know what is going on.

A more general piece of advice offered by some retired academics to future retirees was that they should accept retirement when it came. Those retirees viewed retirement as a natural part of the life course, as a phase of life that should be accepted and not dreaded. Part of this meant coming to grips with and making peace with the possibility of declining energy and abilities as the retirement years went on. Most of the retired academics seem to have accepted this new phase of life with equanimity and without a sense of crisis, perhaps reflecting their sense of satisfaction about earlier achievements. They would agree with their colleague, a seventy-four-year-old professor of German from the research university, who summed up his reactions to retirement: "I didn't notice any psychological depression. I didn't anticipate it with any great horror. And when it came, I accepted it without any feeling of being let down or anything. The sun still shone. A colleague of mine asked me one time, 'Was it brutal?' I said, 'Not in the least.'"

Although not all of the academics were thrilled by their retired status, most of them did in time come to accept retirement and recommended this acceptance to others. A seventy-eight-year-old male research university economist spoke up for coming to terms with retirement:

> One thing that strikes me in talking to colleagues who've retired, I know some of them who almost refuse to make the adjustment. I think that the future retiree ought to sort of keep in mind that this, after all is said and done, is a new way of life. And you ought to make up your mind that you have to adjust to a new way of life. I know one colleague, for example, who has been retired longer than I, who hasn't yet made the adjustment. And in talking to him I get the impression that the one thing he misses the most is that he cannot walk into a classroom and be in command. He misses that. I think the future retiree ought to keep in mind that he can no longer do that, and so what. You don't have to be in command. If you are in command of what you have in your own mind, this is enough, it seems to me. So this is my broad generalization. And this is the same as saying, "Don't fight it. It's coming; you know it's coming." It's a new way of life; retirement is a new way of life. Why fight it?

In the words of a British male engineer, aged seventy-two: "I would certainly advocate making a complete break. You live in the past if you don't. This is a chance for a new lease on life."

Although he had initially resisted retirement, acceptance was also advised by this British male retiree, aged sixty-eight, from the faculty of education:

You see, I didn't want to retire. That's why I stayed on as long as I could. I enjoyed the job. I was afraid of being a back number, I suppose, and being regarded as one. I had an idea in my mind that once you retire, people no longer take notice of you. And so I postponed it as long as possible. So I think my advice to anybody else now who has retired is that retirement is not so bad after all. Take it and enjoy it. Get on with it.

A research university home economist, aged sixty-eight, saw retirement as part of the general aging process. In her opinion, changes associated with aging should be accepted, not dreaded:

I feel as if a lot of people's problems is that they dread old age and don't face old age as one of the normal phases of life. This may be very unpleasant to the majority of people and it isn't exactly attractive to me. But I said when I was sixty years old that I felt like I had lived my life. And one of my friends who had ten children, some of them still growing up, said, "Aren't you fortunate." I think another thing that has helped me that other people don't have is because I wasn't married. I came back here to do something for these four elderly relatives. I have seen each one of them fail and change and depart this life. I think this helps make a person realistic.

A final suggestion offered to future retirees concerned moving or not moving from the preretirement community. Some retired academics advocated moving away after retirement, whereas others advocated staying; however, a piece of advice offered by a research university home economist, aged sixty-seven, during her preretirement interview was worth considering by all: "I really don't believe that people should move right away. I did for a while, but I've come to the conclusion that you better take a year to sort of sort yourself out and see where you're going to go before you make any abrupt change in your lifestyle. And that's the main thing."

A sixty-four-year-old liberal arts college musician gave his ideas on why people should not move after retiring:

We're very comfortable in our house and we've known people who in retiring in the past had sold off their house and moved into an apartment or had moved away from four seasons to a more temperate kind of climate. I have never really talked to anybody really seriously that I've known well who hadn't regretted making that move. Until they really get to a point where keeping up a house and a yard and where they maybe have more space than they need. We have more space than we really need, but we enjoy it. We enjoy being here. We have not felt like moving away.

Other academics, like these male British retirees, a computer scientist, aged sixty-two, and a theologian, aged seventy, advised staying in place because of the proximity to one's university:

Well, for a person of my temperament, it would be absolutely fatal to move away from the university. There are some people that may want to, but for me, I've been here for thirty-five years, so the university is very important to me. So it would be fatal for me to move away. I prefer this environment so that I can keep in touch. I think anyone who makes a complete break is taking a big risk. I don't think they know what they are getting themselves into. So staying in the same house, the same place, and exactly the same university, that would be my advice.

Well, that's a little bit presumptuous because people now are very different in what they feel they've got to do academically. If you want to continue work, then you must be near the library. You can't move to a rural area. That seems to be one very obvious point. Some people have just had enough of it after so long. In my case, it's quite obvious that I must stay near the library, which is exceptional here.

Those academics who recommended moving away from the pre-retirement community also had valid reasons. Some recommended moving in order to enjoy a new retirement lifestyle. For instance, a comprehensive university physical scientist, aged eighty-two, talked about the advantages of his planned retirement community and encouraged new retirees to try it: "I would suggest they come to Sun City. Because Sun City is a city that's built for retirement. Did you know that?"

Other academics who had moved away since retiring, like this male research university professor of French and secondary education, aged seventy-two, recommended moving to a place that would encourage a more healthy lifestyle: "Look to your health! Choose a retirement spot conducive to healthful living and year-round outdoor activity." Health was also on the mind of a liberal arts college professor of religion and philosophy, aged seventy-six, when he advised moving closer to family members because of the risk of health problems with advancing age: "Well, you have to work on your health, I think. That's one thing. If they have family and the relationship is strong, I think you should be nearby them as people get older. Both for their own sake and the sake of those who are close to them. When you get up in years, you're going to need supervision and care, and that sort of thing needs to be thought out."

And a male British historian, aged seventy-seven, talked about the important issue of planning a move carefully so as to avoid the complication of additional moves as one grew older and more frail: "Acquire a house in a new area of choice several years before retirement and visit it during vacations. This enables one to get to know the neighborhood at all times of the year, to make friends, acquire local contacts, and become part of the new environment before leaving the old. Avoid the need to make a second move as one grows older."

The final reason some retired academics gave for suggesting moving away from the preretirement community centered on the norm of noninterference. In essence, a number of the academics were concerned about the possibility of retirees involving themselves too much — indeed, meddling — in the affairs of their department or school when they were no longer active. The best strategy, they reasoned, might be simply to move away. Two British male retirees, a seventy-six-year-old obstetrician and gynecologist and a seventy-seven-year-old dentist, gave their thoughts on this issue:

I am convinced it was wise to cut adrift from my work immediately I retired, and to move away. I recall when I first took up my duty there my predecessor, a man of the utmost distinction and charm, paid frequent visits to me, took up a great deal of my time, offered me advice which when I accepted it sometimes got me into disfavor with other colleagues, and so on. I didn't wish to subject my successor to this sort of thing. More important, however, I did not wish to be tortured by observing his youthful and vigorous successes in fields of activity in which I had become discouraged.

Oh, well, they say this place will never be the same without you. Of course, it won't be the same because your face won't be there, but things will go on, you know, immediately, the moment you're out of here. But I still go back; I still enjoy it. But when I did finish my work, I thought we musn't go back and get under the feet of other people. You must go back to your place only just on a social visit, to talk. But I don't think we should get involved. I don't think that you are anything but an embarrassment, in general terms.

Their American colleague, a seventy-eight-year-old research university economist, summed up how he thought one should act after retiring — one should belong, but not belong:

The other thing I say is that the future retiree ought to make up his mind that he's got no business poking his nose into departmental meetings, asking what this committee is doing and objecting to some changes in the graduate program. You're out of it. Sit back and observe it. Keep in touch, surely. I have a sense of belonging and not belonging. Not belonging in the sense that I expect to exercise any influence, but belonging in the sense that here after all is a great big family. I'm still a member of it, even though I happen to be retired.

Continuing Work

"I have never been happy unless I am producing something,

my scholarly work. If you have worked hard all your life, you

must continue your work."

a seventy-year-old male professor of history

In previous chapters, we saw that retired academics were pleased to have time to spend on what they liked professionally after retiring, that they suggested continuation of professional work during retirement to others who were not yet retired, and that they sometimes made retirement migration decisions based on opportunities to continue their professional work. In this chapter, we turn to what the retired academics saw as their own professional strengths during their preretirement careers, how they utilized those strengths in professional activities during retirement, and how they viewed the opportunity structure available for continuing their work. We also look at how the academics were able to keep current in their fields during the retirement years.

The retirees were asked a number of questions about their professional involvements during retirement. These questions involved the extent of their participation both in professional roles such as teaching, research or other creative work, consulting, or academic administration after retiring and in specific professional activities such as reading journals in their field, attending professional meetings, publishing chapters, books, and articles, or producing other creative works such as art or musical compositions. Retirees were also asked to talk about their special professional strengths during their careers prior to retirement and the age they believed they had done their best professional work, in order to better understand their continued professional engagement in retirement.

First, it is important to point out that a large majority of the academics across institutions in both the United States and the United Kingdom continued to be involved in professional pursuits after they retired from their college or university. As might be expected, professional participation was very high among the most recently retired academics. For example, a full 92 percent of professors in the research university longitudinal transition to retirement study said they were continuing professional roles such as teaching, research, or consulting at the end of one year of retirement. Professional role participation was also high, however, among academics who had been retired for longer periods; overall, at least four-fifths of the retirees in both the United States and the United Kingdom said they had engaged in at least one professional role (e.g., teaching, research or other creative work, consulting) at some time during their retirement, thus showing high levels of professional role continuity during the retirement years. Furthermore, at least one-half of the retired academics, with the exception of the liberal arts college retirees, said they had engaged in professional roles in the past year, with about one-third of retirees being paid for those activities. Among newly retired academics in the transition to retirement study, one-half of the retirees were receiving a salary or fees for their postretirement professional activities one year after retiring.

There were some interesting differences among retirees from the various types of institutions regarding professional activities during retirement. Liberal arts college professors were the most likely to have continued teaching, with about three-fifths having done so at some time during their retirement. Although fewer research university (nearly one-half) and old civic university (about two-fifths) retirees had continued teaching after retiring, the number of academics from those institutions who continued teaching was still substantial.

Comprehensive university retirees were the least likely to have continued teaching, with only about one-third having taught at some time during their retirement. Conversely, research university and old civic university retirees were the most likely to have continued research or other creative work; about two-thirds of retired academics from those institutions continued their research or other creative work during the retirement years. A considerable proportion (about one-half) of liberal arts college and comprehensive university retirees, however, also continued research or other creative work. Consulting was less common among the retired academics than was either teaching or research and was engaged in most frequently by old civic university and research university retirees (40 percent and 33 percent, respectively). Only a handful of academic retirees continued administrative roles in retirement, probably reflecting the limited opportunities available.

Reading journals and attending meetings were two important ways that the retired academics were able to keep up with their fields. A large majority of retired academics from all types of institutions in both countries continued to read professional journals in their field. Research university and old civic university retirees were most likely to continue to attend professional meetings (about two-thirds); in contrast, liberal arts college retirees were least likely to continue to do so (about one-fourth). Comprehensive university retirees occupied an intermediate position, with about one-half of those retirees continuing to attend professional meetings. With respect to continued scholarly productivity after retiring, the research university and old civic university retirees were the most likely to continue publishing journal articles during retirement. Additionally, the British old civic university retirees were more likely to continue publishing books and chapters than were American professors from any type of institution, thus continuing publication patterns established earlier during their preretirement careers.

Professional Strengths during the Preretirement Career

When the retired academics were asked to describe what they considered to be their special professional strengths during their careers prior to retirement, retirees across colleges and universities in both the United States and the United Kingdom were more likely to identify teaching as their major professional strength than to identify any other professional role. Liberal arts college and comprehensive university retirees, however, were the most likely to say that teaching and curriculum development were their main strengths; in comparison, research university and old civic university retirees were more likely to say that both teaching and research were professional strengths.

A number of liberal arts college retirees, including an eighty-three-year-old mathematics professor and a seventy-eight-year-old English professor, both females, and their male colleague, a seventy-nine-year-old political scientist, described their strength in teaching based on the positive feedback they had received from students:

Apparently, from what students tell me, I was able to get things across in a clear way. I think especially in mathematics; it was my forte. And then, I was always willing to help students. My brother was in California at a meeting and he ran into a man who had been at my college. Well, he told my brother that he would never have gotten through mathematics if it hadn't been for me. So you can see, that's where my strength was.

Well, from what students say to me, I think the commonest remark I hear from alumni, who are not particular friends, you know, just run of the mill students is "She certainly made us work." I regard that as a compliment.

Oh, I would say effectiveness in the classroom. When I retired, they gave me a party. Students liked me in spite of the fact that I think I was one of the hardest graders that they had. I insisted on their measuring up. Students appreciate that, too.

Research university retirees likewise talked about teaching as a strength and as a source of satisfaction, as illustrated by the responses of a sixty-five-year-old rhetoric professor and his seventy-year-old colleague in radiology, both males:

Well, I think I got along well with students and that this has made me a much better teacher. Understanding them and their problems and satisfactions has helped a great deal in shaping my teaching. I think that I have been a successful teacher and that's my main source of satisfaction. I haven't been a very good researcher. Our field is not proving susceptible to much research of the kind I'm interested in, and so that part has been disappointing.

I think that my biggest contribution has been to give our students an appreciation of the academic heritage that they are about to inherit. An appreciation of radiobiology that has gone on before they got into the business. Pointing out areas where there's still lots of work to be done. And having given them an appreciation of scientific heritage, then give them an opportunity to go, and encourage them to take a fall and go. Watch them develop. I have not dictated what they should do, but pointed out opportunities and let them go.

For some academics, like this sixty-nine-year-old English professor from the same university, teaching involved a great deal of innovation and the creation of new programs. The writing programs that he developed became internationally acclaimed.

I think I was a good teacher. I love teaching. I brought them texts they never heard of before. Although I did not sense this consciously, that my job was to be an innovator, not to continue being a good teacher of the standard books. But to invent new things, introduce new texts they never heard of before, invent a new program like the writers' workshop. Not just a writing class, but all kinds of seminars around it. Then I started this program with my wife, the international program. And together we started the translation series, which publishes book after book after book. My job was to do new things that hadn't been done before. Basically, I'm a poet who had to become practical. I had to combine those two parts of life.

For other academics, teaching centered on the training of advanced graduate students, who would in turn become the next generation of academics. The words of a research university physiology and biophysics professor, aged sixty-five, communicated pride in the Ph.D. students he had produced over the years:

Basically training others. I had seventeen graduate students of my own and I was active in research with them. I'm very proud that three that come to mind instantly are executives in other departments in prestigious locations in the United States. I suppose I only could consider two of them as not having lived up to their potential.

Many retirees, on the other hand, especially those from the American research university and the British old civic universities, spoke of their own research or other creative work as their main professional strength during their careers prior to retirement. The comments of a sixty-nine-year-old male British electronic engineer conveyed the great pleasure that those academics derived from their own scholarly and creative pursuits:

Well, I suppose I should gauge that by thinking of the degrees to which I have enjoyed these different things. Without any question, I have enjoyed the research more than anything else, and then perhaps after that, the writing. I never regarded myself as being a brilliant teacher. I have tried to do my best with the students. But in my case, without any doubt, I have enjoyed the research more than anything. I miss the work.

His colleague, a seventy-six-year-old British physician, also spoke of his strength as a researcher, which he saw as continuing indefinitely:

The best part of my research came much later in life than most people. Most people do their best research when they're thirty or forty. But I was very immature. I did some of my best research in my late forties. I could do research until I'm one hundred!

Some of the retirees went on to describe their own particular research strengths in detail. Two American research university male retirees, a child psychiatrist aged seventy-five and an energy engineer aged seventy-two, shared this information about their research specialties:

Before my retirement, I had written the section on diagnoses of children for DSM-II, the revised diagnostic and statistical manual of the American Psychiatric Association. My concepts, part of them at least, are in the ICD-IX, the International Classification of Disease. In terms of the initial grouping, they put all of the conduct disorders together in one classification, to which I objected; that has now been accepted. So I've seen my ideas accepted more. The thing that I think is most important is the classification of the disorders of childhood. The special strengths relating to that are: one, an orientation to child psychiatry; and two, some feeling for, and capacity to use, statistical methods. I just learned recently that an early paper of mine on clustering is now always cited, I was told.

Well, I went to the Midwest because of the institute of hydraulic research there, which was unique in the country, and it's become so, more or less, in the world. I didn't go for the university, I didn't go for the town, but for the institute of hydraulic research. And that was the essential tie. It was a field of specialization. I had studied it in Europe. I had worked at MIT and Columbia and at Caltech in that field, and I came here as a professor and a member of this research institute.

Academics who were involved in creative endeavors such as music and art obviously described very different kinds of strengths than did those who worked in scientific fields. In talking about their artistic accomplishments, a sixty-eight-year-old liberal arts college musician and a seventy-one-year-old research university artist, both males, explained what their creative work involved:

I was constantly a pianist. I am also a composer, you know. I composed a great deal, and last year my ballet was performed. I have written quite a bit. And you see, I did not want to involve myself overwhelmingly with teaching because I always feel as a pianist and a composer that I have to continue that work. You can pass it on.

I had a lot of time at the university to work. I came out there as a visiting artist. You know, when you talk to painters, they have different problems all the time. We work at the easel and you have many aesthetic ideas, problems in painting that you're involved with, and these problems are what you are concerned with. I'm a painter.

A much smaller number of retired academics talked about academic administration as their professional strength than talked about either teaching or research. In describing his administrative abilities, a recently retired research university writer, aged sixty-nine, said: "I turned out to be an excellent choice as director of the writers' workshop. I did a good job here." Similarly, an eighty-eight-year-old male liberal arts college economist said: "I think that I was a pretty intelligent guy. I became dean of the college." And a sixty-nine-year-old research university dean of liberal arts fleshed out the requisites of the administrative role by talking about both his accomplishments and his responsibilities as dean:

> Administration was my first responsibility. I am the kind of person who believes in being in the office before eight in the morning and always, of course, being available until five or thereabouts in the afternoon. I like to think I was a pretty good teacher when I was over here, but let's face it, I spent the last thirty years of my professional career in administration. The variety of activities and responsibilities associated with the liberal arts deanship appealed to me. For the most part, I'd have to say that relationships with faculty were very satisfying, and so to have the opportunity to work with them was the most satisfying aspect of the job. When I first came into the office, there was a lot of faculty dissatisfaction with the curriculum, especially with the general education program, which had been adapted while many of us were away during World War II, and that took four or five years to unravel, shall we say. And then, of course, there was always the problem of relationships with the legislature and getting the amount of money that we felt we needed. And then, during the sixties, the problems of the dissenters, you know. So it varied; but I'd have to say that each period had its particular challenges.

Some retired academics also spoke of clinical work as their particular professional strength. Those academics were most frequently from medicine or other health-related professions and considered patient care and education to be important aspects of their careers. Commitment to such clinical work was reflected in the words of a seventy-year-old female physician who was about to retire from the research university: "Giving patients who deal with chronic disease enough education to deal with their problems most of the time themselves, but the security of knowing that there will be prompt response if needed. Teaching students to do the same."

Her British medical colleague, a pediatrician aged seventy-four, described how he had helped build up clinical services in his city:

> My main interest within pediatrics was in cardiology, and I and my colleagues built up the cardiological services here from nothing, the pediatric cardiological services. So I am particularly interested to know what's happening at the Children's Hospital. So that was a special interest of mine while I was active and remains so. While I was there, I regarded one of the functions of the university department, being a medical department, as playing a part in building up hospital services which the hospitals themselves, and the National Health Service as such, would perhaps have found it difficult to do. For instance, when I first started, I wanted to help with the development of services; for a time I put one of my lecturers onto the cardiology service, and she in fact played a very active part in this. When the services had been built up by the university to a certain point, then one was able to say to the hospital authorities, "Look, you've been receiving this service for nothing from the university and it's about time you paid a consultant to do it all." Which is what happened.

Also in the context of professional strengths, we asked the retired academics at what age they believed they had done their best professional work. This included teaching, research, and any other academic activities they were engaged in. Interestingly, most of the academics felt that their best work had been done in middle age, during either their forties or their fifties. A smaller number believed that their best work was done during their thirties, and an even smaller number said their best work was done either from age sixty to retirement or after retirement.

We turn now to look at how the retired academics utilized the professional strengths they had built up and honed over their long careers in continuing professional activities during the retirement years. The retirees were involved extensively in professional roles and activities during retirement, indicating their continued interest in and dedication to their fields.

Continuing Research or Other Creative Work

There were generally more opportunities for the academics to continue scholarly and other creative activities during retirement than there were to continue teaching activities. Retired academics from virtually all disciplines talked about the pleasure of having full time, if they chose, to focus on the research questions and creative endeavors that they formerly had to juggle with other parts of their professional lives prior to retirement. Typical of academics who continued their research was the British old civic university historian cited in the quotation at the beginning of this chapter, who said that in order to be happy he had to produce something. And to him, producing something during retirement meant continuing his scholarly productivity. His colleague, a seventy-four-year-old psychologist, also spoke of continuing his work: "Personally, I decided I would make writing my main activity when I retired." Similar thoughts were expressed by an American academic, a seventy-year-old male research university zoologist: "I find that it's very nice to have full-time for research. Of course, I've tried to remain active. And to me there's been very little change other than meeting class, which I didn't have a very big interest in anyway."

The kinds of research and scholarly activity that the academics pursued in retirement were as varied and impressive as were their preretirement careers. Retirees of both sexes, all ages, and across colleges and universities pursued their individual creative paths. Illustrating the work of the scientists, these research university retirees, an eighty-five-year-old female pediatrics professor and two males, a seventy-one-year-old dentistry professor and a seventy-three-year-old biochemistry professor, described their research activities:

There is a fascination about going into the unknown and finding out things that will be useful to help other people. You feel you've done something and you've seen that what you've done has been of help in some chronic disease or something. I think therefore that research is one of the most satisfying types of work. You can actually see what you've accomplished.

I'm still doing it. I have a grant I'm working on. I just started it in this past year or so. That's keeping me busy. I was working on it even before I got the grant. My wife is working on it too.

The only thing that retirement did for me in terms of my profession was that I no longer taught. Beyond that, there hasn't been any change. I come to work in the lab at nine o'clock in the morning and I leave about four o'clock in the afternoon. Of course, this whole operation depends on the National Science Foundation. That is, they supply the money, and without their grants, we pretty well collapse. So you have to apply to the National Science Foundation. So far, we've been successful, though we haven't gotten as much money as we would like to have. By March or whatever it is, we have to reapply. So, hopefully, they'll see fit to continue the grant. But each two years you face a deadline, and you can have the rug pulled out from under your feet.

A recently retired research university professor of mechanics and hydraulics, aged seventy-one, said:

My time spent on research problems has actually increased. I am the principal investigator on one research contract, which supports two student assistants, and contribute to another, which supports my two other graduate students. I am still writing papers for publication and participating in national and international professional meetings.

Retired academics representing the humanities were likewise engaged in a wide variety of projects, a sample of which are presented here. A British old civic university economic historian, aged sixty-nine, for example, had been commissioned to write a history:

When I retired, I was given the job of writing the history of the university. So I have this room and access to all the records. I come in two or three times a week, sometimes more. There have been a number of histories dealing with particular periods. And then there has been one general history dealing with the whole period of the university, that is from 1851 to 1951, but that is generally considered now to be (a) inadequate and (b) out-of-date, you see.

Things have moved on. A certain amount of new material has come to light.

A seventy-five-year-old American research university professor of Spanish and Portuguese had received a Guggenheim fellowship since retiring to help support his research: "I have been productive since retirement. As a matter of fact, I had my Guggenheim fellowship after I retired. I published a very well-received book, which was singled out by *Choice* magazine as one of the outstanding academic texts of 1976."

And two humanities retirees, a speech professor, aged ninety-five, and an English professor, aged ninety-six, described in touching terms how they were still trying to continue working in their scholarly specialties several decades after their retirement from the research university:

I worked harder after retirement than ever before. I wrote books about debate and communication. I'd like to write more on linguistics. My career is a succession of heavy labor right through.

I frankly don't remember those years between sixty-five and seventy, except for research. Yes. I did some this morning. The secret is to have a goal later in life. I still want to rewrite Chaucer, though I've done much. I think what I am doing is up to my very best standard. I hope I'm not boasting.

The social scientists spoke of being engaged in a wide variety of enterprises — everything from conducting surveys to writing books in their fields of expertise. A psychologist from the research university's institute for child development, aged seventy-six, described the key role she had played in work on the Head Start program:

The first thing I did was to do a survey of the kinds of day care that children under thirteen were receiving here and the kind of households in which they lived and the attitudes that parents had. I was particularly interested in studying the households, the homes in which mothers worked. This was fairly extensively done. We trained hundreds of people drawn from a variety of clubs and departments and people who were interested in interviewing, and we covered every single household. This took the better part of two years, really, to do. I was trying to get reliable information for setting up a government-supported day care here, and as a result of that the Head Start which we now have was the first all-day day care in the state. After that, I was actually doing consultant work in the Head Start program throughout the country. Now I am interested in what is happening to children who need care while their mothers are working right here. So I am still working; I have a project going on right now.

Two male political scientists, both aged seventy-one, one from a liberal arts college and the other from the research university, described the books they were working on in retirement:

> While I was still teaching, the last couple of years, I began working on the preparation of a textbook that was a collaborative effort with three other men. That came out in 1976 or 1977; I have to check the date. It was published by John Wiley. It was for an introduction to political science course, the beginning course. And it did quite well, so a revised edition is now, well it's completed, and I'm waiting for the galley proofs. They should come any day. I wrote two chapters for this book. One was on political philosophy; the role of political philosophy in political science, primarily on the traditional and historical point of view. It reviewed the whole history of political thought from ancient times to the present. The other chapter was on legal systems, primarily Anglo-American.

> I began planning five years ago a retirement project — a textbook, an introduction to politics. I'm continuing research and writing fully. In fact, that's the main occupation. I'm set up at home with a computer and printer and a floppy disk system, so I can put out nice stuff without any secretarial help. I just printed up this 380-page manuscript at home.

Academics who were creative artists often needed little in the way of college or university facilities or support to continue their work. A retired artist and former research university museum director, aged seventy-one, described his lifetime commitment to painting: "The rewards are from doing the work, not having it be known. Art professors have more time for their own work. There is little preparation for tests, et cetera. Art must be collected as well as produced. It must be transmitted."

His female colleague, also aged seventy-one, explained how the work she was doing on mosaics in North Africa bridged the arts and the humanities:

> This is what my heart is really in. We're working now on our latest publication. We've been doing, and I may even start another project working on these mosaics, and then of course publishing the results. At the moment we're trying to finish publishing all the work that we've done up to this point, because it's a combination of archaeological art and historical approaches. And it takes an enormous amount of time to get everything together and then you realize there are things you have to check up on, and so you have to go back and do this. Which for us sometimes means making a few new diggings in the ground, which of course can bring some answers that can also raise new questions. And then the whole process of getting it ready for publication is enormous, because for the first volume I had an editorial assistant. For this volume I haven't had one, so I've had to do it. And you know, you can keep thinking, "All right, it really is ready now," and it can be months before you can really get it to the printer, because you've got to do all your proofreading, your typesettings and more proofreading. Even still, after one, two, three, four, five, six, yes six, books, I still can't judge properly. Then there's always the unexpected things. For example, my colleague in Tunisia has had, within this last grant we had, has had two children. She now has three. She was named director of the major museum in Tunisia. So, there went whole blocks of time, particularly when I was in Tunisia.

Although most of the retired academics recognized that there are multiple pathways to living a successful life in retirement and that there are also many ways to continue to contribute to society, some had no patience for their colleagues who chose not to continue with their scholarly activities. This male British university pathologist, aged eighty-three, questioned the interest and commitment of those academics who did not continue their work in retirement:

I should say that during retirement you should be able to carry on with your work. Anybody who doesn't want to go on working after they've officially retired, they should have never started that job. I mean, medicine is the only thing worth doing, isn't it? Anybody who wants to stop medicine, and I've met people who have, they've never been very interested in it in the first place. I should say they've been looking forward to retirement for years, and then they drop out. They should have dropped out thirty or forty years earlier.

A newly retired American research university professor of preventive and community dentistry, aged seventy-one, gave a reason close to home for his not dropping out — a role model within the family kept him working!

No, I think my case is a little unusual in that I do have a role model in my father-in-law. My wife's father is a retired professor at the University of California. He's eighty-five years old and still goes in to his office every day and continues his research. I guess I have a good role model.

Continuing Teaching

Many retired academics not only continued their research or other creative work, but found opportunities for teaching during the retirement years. The fields in which they continued to teach were spread across the disciplines, as was the case for research or other creative work. Some retirees found teaching opportunities at their home institutions, whereas others went farther afield in order to continue teaching. This liberal arts college retiree, a sixty-six-year-old astronomer, was able to continue to teach one course each year in his specialization at his college. This man also continued to direct the planetarium at his institution, which meant involvement in additional educational programs.

You ask me why I'm still teaching. Why, I just enjoy it. Apparently I have the ability to popularize science endeavors. In other words, I think I have been able to interpret the astronomical phenomena and the space program, and I have sufficient background in it so I can interpret this for the general public.

Another liberal arts college retiree, a philosopher aged seventy-five, described a brief extension of teaching at his college: "There was a one-year extension in active teaching, which I voluntarily reduced to two-thirds the time of service; that is, permitting one quarter."

University retirees, like this male British old civic university anatomist, aged seventy-five, and female American research university home economist, aged sixty-eight, also found opportunities for teaching at their home institutions:

I must say that I would be lost if I wasn't able to come in here. I haven't much in the way of outside pursuits. I'm not particularly interested in research. I made it clear when I came back that all I really wanted to do was teach. And I just carried on doing that. I also work in the dissecting room. Because all the time I'm teaching anatomy, I'm pointing out the relevance of it. I give them a preview of what they're going to run into. It's important to link what you're doing with clinical stories.

I do like associations with students. Teaching this off-campus course really did a lot to put me in shape for everything. This one little requirement, you know, a class once a week, the preparation you have to make for that, trying to meet the needs of students, and the interests of students. It's a hangover from the kind of routine that you're accustomed to. I enjoy it very much. And I think it helps a person with everything. I have taught three successive semesters now. The first time I did this was in the Saturday and Evening program. I like the students you get in classes like that. They are mature in general, and they have a purpose. They are people who are on the job and they have some need for this information. I've been asked to write this course up as a correspondence course, and it's been accepted.

But many academics who continued teaching after retiring taught in contexts other than their home institutions. Three women retirees, a seventy-two-year-old music professor, a sixty-eight-year-old foreign language professor, both from the liberal arts colleges, and a seventy-two-year-old physical education professor from the research university, used their teaching skills to work with different populations than the college and university students they had worked with during their preretirement careers:

> I am teaching still; it's just younger people than I did teach. I am still teaching music, mostly to children.

> I try to live what I believe. It means to give back free all the gifts you had that were given to you. For me, this was foreign languages. I used this my whole life to earn my living, and now I give it free to youth who want to learn foreign languages. Free of charge. Only to serious, willing students who want to learn a language, and I give this to them. Especially to children from good Christian families, from big families who cannot afford lessons. I will do this as long as I can do it.

> I head up the Institute of Lifetime Learning for AARP, and I teach in that all the time except when I'm down in Florida. I do professional teaching there; that is, exercise, relaxation, activities in the water, and so on, geared to the elderly. I teach anywhere from two to, I guess, six hours has been the most I've had when some of the things overlapped. I've done some speaking. I just got back recently from Nebraska, where I did a seminar for them on research and publication.

Another woman, an opera coach aged eighty-six who had formerly taught at a liberal arts college, talked about her move to New York after retiring and the kind of teaching she did there:

> With music, with private lessons, if you have the reputation for being able to help people, it's a little like being a good doctor; you can go on forever. It will be twenty-one years this fall that I've been in New York. I had a very distinguished professional pupil doing a lot of concerts and opera work — he sang with Sutherland and people of that type — and he said he'd tried a lot of teachers and none of them seemed to help him as much as I did, and why didn't I come to New York and he'd guarantee me pupils. So I did what he suggested. Five of my former students who had graduated followed me to New York, so I had a nucleus to begin with, you see, which is very lucky.

For a number of retirees who continued teaching activities, opportunities arose at colleges and universities other than where they had taught prior to retirement. These opportunities occurred both in their own country and abroad. A research university speech professor, aged ninety-five, who chose not to be tape-recorded, recalled his teaching experiences until age eighty-five at the Universities of Missouri, Mississippi, California, and Southern Illinois, during which he said he worked harder than ever before. Several peripatetic male academics, including a British old civic university historian, aged seventy-four, an American research university ophthalmologist, aged seventy-six, and an American comprehensive university economist, aged sixty-four, described their teaching experiences in numerous places:

I have been teaching in American colleges and universities. But it's my own desire to continue teaching, which I like doing. It gives a certain satisfaction to go on meeting young people at that sort of level where you can communicate something to them. I don't do as much teaching in America as I did as head of department here. I may say that I started at a small college, not at the university. I taught for four semesters, that is two years, at a college in Maryland. That is a small college which is run on liberal arts lines but is financed by the state. It's to some extent experimental in that respect. I could have gone on teaching there regularly, but I began to feel that I didn't want to, so I made an arrangement that I would come back most second semesters. And I did that, and then in 1979 I went to Ann Arbor for a semester. I taught one semester at the college in 1981–82, and then this year I've been doing writing. I have done very well, as far as America has been very good to me. I find that they are very kind to me at the college, and I teach two courses and small classes. I teach the first part of the colonial period up to 1660. There is a special reason for having me there, and that is that it's on the site of the first capital of Maryland and there is a big archaeological historical program associated with this. I do informally work with the commission and so I am, in a sense, their historical adviser on the early part of the era of the seventeenth century. I know something about it; I'm not a specialist in America. They have a very fine historian on their staff, and she and I work together on day-long projects connected to, for example, organizing a conference next May on seventeenth-century Maryland. But I don't intend to do this indefinitely; it depends on what's going on. I also teach correspondence on the expansion of Europe and sometimes I teach a course on British history as well.

I like the teaching. I am teaching in quite a few places. I am doing what I did here; I teach residents of ophthalmology in basic courses of ophthalmology. I teach in about, I would say, six or seven courses. I teach here; I'll be here at the beginning of May. Then I go to Indianapolis and teach there in the medical school. In the beginning of the year I go to San Juan, Puerto Rico, for three weeks, and that has been going on for more than ten years. I became a member there of the faculty before I retired. Then I go to make the rounds during the year. Now my schedule includes usually here, even twice a year, then Indianapolis, the University of Colorado at Denver. The best courses, I would say, are the longest courses, like Harvard University and others. We have been having a course for many years in Maine; there we have about one hundred and sixty doctors. I am part of the long basic course; I have a week, up to two weeks, three weeks, and that's about the maximum in one course. I go to Stanford University too, after Maine.

I give lectures here and other places. Since I retired, I've delivered lectures in Korea, Southeast Asia, Australia, and New Zealand with Sensa, which is an organization of central banks in Southeastern Asia, which I've enjoyed. Also, lectures sponsored by the Humanities Board.

For academics who continued to live in their preretirement communities after retiring, there were sometimes opportunities for involvement in less formal teaching activities than classroom instruction. One of these teaching activities was serving as a member of dissertation committees, at least at doctoral-granting institutions. Dissertation committee work was more common among the recent retirees, like this male geologist, aged sixty-six, who spoke of being able to serve on, but no longer direct, doctoral dissertations: "I am still on doctoral dissertation committees, but it's somewhat in passing, or somewhat informal compared to what I have done."

A professional role related to the teaching function that exists in the United Kingdom but rarely in the United States is the role of external examiner. In that role, an academic from one institution reads examinations from other institutions and also participates in the evaluation of graduate theses and dissertations from other institutions in both the United Kingdom and other nations, particularly in the British Commonwealth. A number of British academics continued to serve as external examiners at all levels of higher education during their retirement. Their duties were explained by three British male academics, a sixty-eight-year-old physician, a sixty-seven-year-old oceanographer, and a sixty-eight-year-old engineer:

> When I was in the university, one of the things one has to do is examine for the final M.B. and that sort of thing. For a time I had continued that. This is something where I wanted sort of to continue the interest. The intention there is to make sure that the standards of the candidates come up to what we might call British standards. And this is something where we have a number of examiners from different countries. We have one from Sweden, one from Finland, and one from Austria, one from Germany, and one from India, as well as from the British Isles, hoping that the standard would be such that it's an international sort of thing. And the other part of teaching is that with these examinations we are trying to teach the local people so that they will eventually take over on the examinations, you see. This interest is sort of a teaching function as well as purely an examination. It's a matter of standards and of trying to get the local people to come up to British university standards.

> I've also been doing some external examining still. I'm an external examiner for South Africa to the bachelor's and master's degrees in oceonography, and I still do one or two Ph.D. theses. I think the idea is to try to see that the standards are the best and not too different from one another.

I do occasionally an external exam for the Ph.D.; for instance, I have an Indian Ph.D. thesis on the table which I have to assess. But I don't seek them out. If they come to me from old friends, I don't think I should refuse them yet. But I will do in the near future if I feel that I am getting so far behind that I cannot assess a thesis properly. I don't know if you are aware of this thing, but British Ph.D. exams are conducted usually by an internal examiner and an external examiner. And it is the opinions of those two examiners together which decide whether or not the candidate is successful. The appointment of an external examiner is usually a faculty matter, and once it's been decided and approved by the faculty, or the appropriate committee thereof, then the external examiner is largely independent. He sends in his independent assessment and it is generally accepted in conjunction with the opinion of the internal examiner. In the case of British Ph.D.s, of course, there is in fact an oral examination conducted by the examiners together. Now, in the case of an Indian thesis, the oral examination is conducted in India, and the external examiner, if he is British or whatever, normally isn't present, because of the cost of the journey and the time. So in this case I will not have the opportunity of examining the candidate personally. I will have to work entirely on the thesis, you see.

Continuing Consulting

Although consulting was not as common as either research or teaching in retirement, a considerable number of the retirees, particularly from the universities, played consulting roles during their retirement. Opportunities to continue consulting were particularly frequent among retired academics in the applied professional fields, most notably health-related fields. The expertise of those retirees was sought on an array of practical problems. A research university pediatrician, aged sixty-nine, described the major consultative role he was currently playing:

The state health department has contracted with the pediatrics department of the university to organize the birth defects institute. And a function is to have a regional genetic consultation service.

The state has been divided into five areas. I am the director of this region's genetic consultation service. For each of the five areas, we will have a genetic consultant. What are the functions of this regional genetic consultant service? One, to spread information about modern genetics among the medical professionals and para-professionals. Two, propagation of medical information among the people of the state. Quite often we are asked by high schools, by junior colleges, to give workshops there and discuss these things. Three, we have contracted to have in five places in the northeastern section of the state three genetic counseling offices. Anyone who has a genetic problem or believes they have a genetic problem can come. We get all the information which is needed to give the consultation, and that can take a lot of work. The service is free of charge. We give them counsel and actively discuss the problem at length. We have purposely a male and a female counselor, because I believe that the male and female have somewhat different approaches to the problem, and we complement each other.

An orthopedist from the same institution, also aged sixty-nine, talked about the consulting he was doing related to his research on backache: "I'm a consultant with a number of areas such as the Veterans' Hospital and vocational rehabilitation state department; the same things I did prior to my emeritus status." His British colleague in orthopedic surgery, aged seventy, likewise described his consulting activities, which were often international:

I went and taught and acted as a consultant in Malaysia. And I visited, also professionally, a lot of India and Singapore. I've got a lot of contacts there. I spent three months in Malaysia, but other places it was more a question of going there three or four weeks at a time.

Two recently retired male research university professors of preventive medicine and environmental health, aged seventy and sixty-three, who participated in the transition to retirement study, described the consulting activities they had engaged in during the past year:

You betcha. I'm building a whole new career for myself. I've established my own consulting firm operating out of my house consulting in the occupational health field. There's litigation that is involved. Of particular interest to me is to provide industrial hygiene and safety services for the small industries, particularly in this state, because of their accessibility.

I find myself doing much the same thing in consulting that I did in teaching. It's just a different audience. I could have a full-time job being a consultant. I do consulting for farm accidents. I go all over the country now. It's exciting. I was limited as to my exposure here. From that point of view, I could run all over the countryside doing all of it. I find that presently I'm being asked to recite what I've been telling everyone for the last twenty-five or thirty years. It's a tremendous confidence builder, that I was right to start with. No one was listening. And now they're paying me to listen, where I gave it to them for free before. I think we're accomplishing something, so in actuality my professional life is just beginning.

Retirees in non-health-related professions, like this British old civic university architect, aged seventy-six, sometimes also found consulting opportunities:

I'm not typical, as I mentioned to you before, really, because I remain in a sense a practicing architect, although only in a very marginal way, in a consulting rather than an administrative capacity. So I'm in touch with professional activities. I keep abreast of what's going on, what's developing with technology, and theories of architecture. So that I'm not out of touch in that way at all. In that way, I have perhaps a greater advantage over many other people who have to break themselves quite off from their academic activities. So that perhaps I'm lucky and there are not a great many people who are in my fortunate position. I keep the contacts still, so I feel I'm alive in architecture. I've been associated with a firm; actually, it's, in this case, it's a firm run by one of my graduates many years ago. I have a link with his office. So if anything comes to me, if people ask me to do a house or do any little comparatively small architecture problem, I bring this into the office. And I am there as a consultant, and his team works out all the executive and administrative side of it. So it relieves me of all the headaches. What is interesting is discussing and making proposals, and doing really quite a bit of designing myself in the early stages of design which is being developed by my younger colleagues in the office. I am continuing in much the same way now in my role as consultant as the position I found myself in when I was involved in practice and teaching.

A British engineer, aged seventy-one, from the other old civic university, found opportunities for consulting at his home institution:

I've chaired university projects, small companies really, engaged in a particular development of the university idea of marketing. The money is given to the university by important groups and foundations to foster bright ideas in the university. The idea is to bring them up to the marketable phase. And the university wishes to be informed of how things are going, and they put in their own chairman of this group of people, and they put me in as chairman not too long ago. I report to the university council. Then there are a number of technical things that crop up; sometimes I do a bit of consulting on a technical problem for a variety of people.

Although much of the consulting engaged in by the retired academics was formal, some retirees also mentioned that they were willing to consult informally on projects for their colleagues. A newly retired research university professor, aged seventy, who was a well-known expert on educational testing, said he was willing to offer his services to anyone who needed them: "Only when people feel that they need help or advice, consulting. I'm not offering it in the sense of forcing it on anyone. Instead, I take exactly the opposite view, that they have the responsibility, and if they have needs, then they know that they are free to contact me."

One important kind of consultation that the academics engaged in during retirement, as they had during their preretirement careers, was editorial work on books and journals. Many of the retirees had been editors or associate editors of journals or served on editorial boards of journals in their field during their careers prior to retirement. Others edited or reviewed books related to their fields. A number of academics were still deeply involved in these editorial activities after retiring. Two British retirees, an eighty-year-old female from the department of Italian studies and a seventy-one-year-old male from the department of botany, spoke of the major editorial responsibilities they currently had:

I am still general editor of the Manchester University Press series of Italian texts — work, unpaid, begun in 1962, which I thoroughly enjoy. The series now has some twenty-three volumes, and editors are still working for me.

Some people find activities in their subject not connected to university work or departmental work. For example, I edit an international journal. It takes lots of work. That's one of my activities. I've been doing that for ten years. It's a joint editorship of two of us. Ninety percent of it is published in English. We publish in English, German, French, and Italian. I also do some consulting.

A female physical educator, aged seventy-one, from the American research university, likewise did major editorial work for a journal:

At the time when I was getting ready to retire, I was offered a chance at a three-year term of editing our research journal for our national association. And I took it. And it was the thing which helped to tide me over, because it was on the deck all the time. There were a large volume of manuscripts, and I was totally responsible for getting the job done on evaluation, et cetera; it is a refereed journal. So I just finished that assignment this summer. When my three-year term ended the first of July on that, I went on to a role which I had had previously, which was an associate editor. The refereed journals have a whole series of review of editors, and I had been on in that role before and simply went into editor-in-chief for those three years, and then I went back in the role of associate editor. I had to go to national meetings in connection with that position as editor.

Some academics, like this female British psychologist, aged seventy-four, did book reviews for journals or other organizations during retirement:

I've done more reviewing since I retired. Again, this is the British Journal of Educational Psychology. They send me books, not very many. The British Council now sends me books to review, maybe two a year. They pay for that. British journals don't pay. The British Council does pay.

Continuing Clinical Work or Practice

As can be expected, it was in the applied professions such as medicine, dentistry, nursing, and social work that retired academics had the opportunity to continue their clinical work or practice in retirement. Two dentists, a sixty-eight-year-old from the American research university and a seventy-seven-year-old from a British old civic university, discussed their clinical practice. The first man continued his practice at his university; the second continued in a nonuniversity setting.

I'm on one day a week; I work all day Tuesday. I come in here on Tuesday morning and this morning I saw twenty-four patients. I knock myself out on Tuesday mornings. On Tuesday afternoon I fill in as instructor of clinical, depending on where I'm needed.

When I qualified in 1927, I continued as a teacher of operative dentistry. Mornings only, nine till one o'clock, six days a week, Saturdays as well. For this I got the princely salary of one hundred and twenty pounds per annum. I was running a practice in the afternoons. It was rather heavy, you know, getting very busy. And I also had a motorcar accident at about this period; I fractured a femur. And this forced me to adjust my life. And I gave up the teaching appointment for a short time, and carried on with the practice. So then I rejoined the teaching staff and eventually became full-time again. Now when I retired in 1965, I had a year without doing any dental work at all. And then I did receive local work. An ex-colleague who had been a student of mine some years before asked me whether I would consider doing scientific work three mornings a week for two months. I never regretted that. I found it very interesting. I then took an offer with two other ex-students of mine, to work at their practice on a special basis, with selected patients. And this I have continued until now, and I miss this. Continuing this emphasis kept me involved in something which, after all, my whole life has mainly been concerned with. The dental trade and treatment of the dental health of the nation.

A newly retired professor of internal medicine, aged seventy, from the research university, also communicated how important it was to her to be able to treat patients after retiring:

The only change I expect to make is to try to work half-time for half the salary I have worked for full-time for years. This will give me a chance to pursue some of my other interests. I think I would find it difficult not to be able to help other people medically when I am still so able to do so.

Also representing the helping professions was a sixty-six-year-old social worker from the same university, who described the considerable demands for her services during her first year of retirement:

I let the social work agencies know that I was available as a girl Friday, and I've had to just call a halt to this year because I've made over the five thousand dollars allowed me for this year. That was a little worrisome to me; whether or not if I wanted to do that, would people use me? And I find that's no problem for me here. It simply is not. In fact, I have had to give notice to Lutheran Social Service. One of their workers left in January, and so they called and said, "Would you fill in?" And I thought, well, maybe six weeks until they find somebody. Well, at the first of April I just said, "This is it; I can't work any longer." And they said, "Well, we would like to keep you." I did a workshop for Lutheran Social Service in the middle of this. I haven't done direct social work practice for seven and one-half years while I was on the faculty. Anyway, I went back and was better than ever. And you don't know that until the client is right there in front of you, and all kinds of problems walk through the door of Lutheran Social Services. And you know, just a variety of human problems. And I had just said jokingly, sort of casually to agency heads, "Well, I think I'll be a social work girl Friday!" And by golly, they took me at my word. I've really had to turn down another job.

Continuing Work in Professional Organizations

Participating in professional organizations in one's field can be an important reflection of commitment both to that field and to colleagues outside of the local college or university community. Many of the academics had been active in various state, national, and international professional organizations during their careers, and some continued their work for those professional organizations during retirement. Major leadership roles were played by an American female liberal arts college sociologist, aged sixty-six, and a British male old civic university dental surgeon, aged sixty-eight, who was currently serving as president of the British Council of Dental Surgeons:

> I'm past president of the state Sociological Society. I am presently on the social implications of science committee of the state Academy of Science.

> The term is for five years, from 1979 to 1984. So my present term is until next year. It is very rewarding. Now, for example, the council is visiting all the medical schools in the country to assess how far their courses meet the standards that have been set. The standards are changing constantly, and we have to decide what to do now. It is a big responsibility. I suppose I spend one full day a fortnight in London.

His colleague, a seventy-year-old British historian, talked about some of the local professional organizations in which he also played a leading role:

> I'm president of a society that promotes the local Cheshire and Lancashire historical publishing societies. The university press publishes for us, you see. I've been president of that society for, what, eleven years, and I'm about to retire from the presidency. It's been very interesting, of course, to be president of the society. These societies and institutions have their meetings, and, of course, I take the chair. The preparation of the business of the meeting is under my direction. This is a special obligation. It's interesting; otherwise, I wouldn't have retained the offices.

Important roles on boards and committees of professional organizations in their fields were played by two male American research university professors, a journalist aged seventy-three and a geologist aged sixty-six, and their female colleague, a nurse aged sixty-six:

I am a member still of the Association for Education in Journalism committee on professional freedom and responsibility, which is one of the three elected committees of that organization. I take a standard part in its meetings; that is, I review reports from the divisions and that sort of thing. In the summer of 1975, I wrote to the executive committee of the Association for Education in Journalism saying that I thought that competence in language skills was, of course, essential for journalism graduates. I felt that it was unsound for the media to be blaming the schools of journalism for doing poor training in this area, because actually the development of adequate language skills should be accomplished in the elementary schools and the secondary schools. And I suggested that the AEJ should set up a program aimed at saying to media everywhere, "Get on the ball; do the job in your own community; it's your job on your newspaper or your station to make sure that your local community is giving its young people an adequate start in life by giving them an adequate level of language skills." This resulted a couple of months later in my being named chairman of a national committee on this topic. Three or four weeks ago, I wrote the draft for the basic letter which the committee will send out to every daily newspaper and probably two thousand stations, a total distribution of six or eight thousand copies, setting out a program of action which could be carried out along these lines.

I am serving as a member of the state preserve board. This takes some time and also involves securing an additional acquaintance with the state. This has been a new thing since my retirement. And over a period of time I intend to acquaint myself with all of the state preserves, the areas that have been designated as preserves, and those that are being considered for preserves. This board had not had a geologist representing that field previously. So I'll probably spend several days a month involved in that.

I've always been an organization person. And right now I have three or four responsibilities in the American Nurses' Association.

I'm an editor of the newsletter for the American Nurses' Association. But I have several activities. I'm a member of the executive committee and a member of a board which is going to establish a credentialing activity for nursing administrators, which was developed by a task force of which I was chairman. It's one of the kinds of things I do very well.

The Opportunity Structure for Continuing Professional Work

Three decades ago, in an early and seminal paper entitled "Organizational Structure and Disengagement: The Emeritus Professor" (*Gerontologist* 7 [1967]: 147–152), Paul Roman and Philip Taietz noted that when the opportunity structure for continued professional activity in retirement is provided by organizations such as colleges and universities the majority of individuals will remain engaged in at least some of the roles they played prior to retirement. In their view, the institutional opportunity structure includes facilities for continued professional work, such as provision of office space, laboratories, libraries, and secretarial assistance, and also an institutional climate that encourages continued interaction with the retiree's departmental and university colleagues. It follows, then, that retirees without a facilitative institutional opportunity structure should have a harder time continuing professional roles than retirees whose institution provides opportunities for continued engagement.

We saw earlier that some of the retired academics said that one of the disadvantages of retirement was not having the facilities and services they needed for remaining professionally involved. Some academics, in contrast, said they were fortunate in having the material supports and the general environment they needed to continue their professional involvements. A research university economics professor, aged seventy-eight, for example, explained how much he appreciated being able to retain an office on campus:

> The retiree ought to request some kind of office space. The fact that you have some place to go; you don't have to go, you go when you want to go. It aids in the adjustment process. You haven't, in other words, cut everything off sharply. The fact that I have an office here, even though I share it with someone, is very important

to me. When I want to come down here and keep up with the literature, I can. Frankly, I'd be lost if I didn't have a place to come down to.

His comments were echoed by a seventy-six-year-old male British anatomist, who said: "I must say that I would be lost if I wasn't able to come in here. I haven't much in the way of outside pursuits."

Some institutions appeared to provide many more opportunities for continued professional engagement than did others and also provided a climate that encouraged continued professional and social interaction more than did others. A comprehensive university astronomer, aged seventy-four, complimented his institution on its efforts on behalf of retirees:

> I'm very happy about that. At my university, a retired professor has all the privileges of an unretired professor. Library, Xeroxing—the physics department even offered to give me a small office and any set of graphic work I wanted done they would take care of, which I have taken advantage of in a few cases where I thought it was pertinent to my profession. I wouldn't do it for personal work, of course. You get full library privileges. You can have indefinite use of all books unless they're called in. The faculty club is very informal and we are always welcome there. We could have the use of a classroom to have meetings if they're school-related. However, pressures from the local business group have forced the university to say that they cannot offer free rooms for meetings to organizations not related to the university. For instance, I tried to set up a meeting for Zero Population Growth and they said they'd have to charge for a room. We have full faculty privileges at the swimming pool and gymnasium. We can still get athletic tickets at greatly reduced prices. We get bulletins about all the concerts and plays and that sort of thing that are going on campus. We always feel welcome when we go back. The social atmosphere on the campus has always seemed to be excellent.

A research university journalism professor and director of publications, aged ninety, also felt included at his university even after many years of retirement: "I feel as much a part of the university as ever; the scholarship, the contact with major administrators. The university has been good to me." And a recently retired British mathematician, aged sixty-six, talked about enjoying both the facilities that were available after retirement and the opportunities for continued involvement in the life of his university:

> It is useful in allowing one the use of library facilities. I find that very useful. The card I was issued expires next September. Presumably I shall have to ask permission for that to be restamped. Or ask permission when that expires to have another card. The reason why I'm hopeful is that I see other people who have been retired several years still using the library. The other thing that I appreciate the university does is to organize, twice a year I suppose, an opportunity for us to visit the university again. I got an invitation in November last year, and it's been renewed again this year, to have lunch in the university. And I found last year that this was an occasion for meeting old friends, but it also allowed us to hear from the vice-chancellor what the present state of things is. So I think that's very helpful. The other occasion is the meeting in May or the lunch in May when the honorary degrees are presented. I think this is confined largely to ex-professors rather than ex-lecturers. I am one of these old fogeys called an emeritus professor.

Retired academics who were not so pleased with their institutional opportunity structure gave advice to their college or university on how to better the situation of academic retirees. In scientific disciplines, lack of adequate laboratories in which to work could be an acute problem. A research university laboratory scientist, aged seventy-two, from the department of preventive medicine, urged support for scientists: "A scientist must be able to work. The university should treat retired professors as not retired in terms of being able to continue their work, especially those who have served long-term."

Retired academics from the United Kingdom, who generally had fewer facilities available than did their American counterparts, offered additional suggestions for a more facilitative opportunity structure. An eighty-two-year-old university physician asked for secretarial assistance, the lack of which was a serious problem for himself and for many of his colleagues: "Having no secretarial assistance, the preparation of typescript has been a sore drudgery. I deeply regret I never learned to type as a young man; I mean to type with accuracy. It's much too late at sixty-five to learn that skill."

Other British academics, like these two male physicians, aged seventy-six and eighty-three, suggested that universities should provide a place where they could work and interact with colleagues:

One day, in his suite with his secretaries, he's got everything at his fingertips; he's got other people doing what he wants. You'll find that the man who suddenly retires wants to keep contact with lots of things, but he's got to write all his letters by hand; he's got to have room in his house to have a study. If he's a scientist, he would like to have somewhere where he can go on with some research. He may be excluded from that. And so he finds himself with very little help. And I would say the first thing that any civilized university should do is to have somewhere where the retired person can relax, can get his letters typed for him; if he is asked by some journal, for instance, to write a paper he can get it typed for him, and he can meet some of his older colleagues or some of his younger ones. But there ought to be a place where the retired man can go and know he can get some secretarial assistance, could get drafts of manuscripts typed for him, and all that sort of thing. That I would think was the hardest. A lot of chaps when they retire just give up. You should be encouraged; you should be given opportunities. The libraries are still open to you, that's true, but it takes a fair amount of mental self-control to go on with that sort of work. I think the university in general treats everyone the same; that's fair. I don't think they treat them well because they don't give them any kind of facilities. They treat them very kindly; they invite them to Christmas dinner and that sort of thing, and public events like honorary degrees, maybe give them honorary degrees. But that's about where it stops. As far as they're concerned, they are quite rightly busy with what they're doing and they forget about you. I still think the absence of any offer of facilities is the worst thing. If you ask the university, you'd know that they'd have to say that would depend on the head of the department; if he's got a room, then you can have it.

I would suggest that all universities ought to have an emeritus building for retired professors and senior lecturers, where they have technical staff to help them. And an office.

The issue of very premature separation from the institutional opportunity structure, particularly for academics who were encouraged or forced to retire early in the United Kingdom during the mid-1980s, was raised by a seventy-six-year-old architect, who offered his suggestions for the continued integration of early retirees:

> Especially nowadays, when people are retiring earlier, early redundancies and so on, is to try and encourage people to retain a link to the university in some way. To invite them to return occasionally in some specific function, to offer them some kind of research link to their ex-department and so on. Universities might think of appointing people who've recently retired to boards. I would think that the university has more of a responsibility in this now that people are being forced into earlier redundancies. They are still very active people. These retirements are coming thick and fast now.

Occasionally a retiree was resourceful enough to be able to utilize the existing institutional opportunity structure, as well as his or her own professional skills, to create an entirely new job that was badly needed within his or her home institution. A seventy-five-year-old research university physician who founded a patient representative program at her university hospital discussed the sequence of events that led to a major new job for her and to an important service role being performed for her university:

> I knew there was something I ought to be doing, but I didn't know what it was. I was really getting uneasy. I just couldn't find in my mind anything that would be meaningful. I got into Project Green and that's fine; I'd been having a back-breaking garden and yard for years and I was interested in that sort of stuff. But in *Time* magazine in the medicine section in September that year, there was an article about a small pilot program that four or five people were trying in one of the metropolitan New York hospitals. There had been a nurse named Nancy McGuire, and I've since come to

know her quite well. She had a piece of heavy equipment fall on her back, and she became a patient in the hospital and was in traction, and she was so taken aback. She was so frustrated about the lack of true communication between what I call the horizontal and the perpendicular people in the hospital. When she got out of the hospital, she talked this over with some of her friends, and four or five of them started a little group and thought they would try it out and see if it were feasible to have a patient representative to articulate those breaks in communication. When I saw that, I knew that was for me, if that were possible. In October, three other members of my staff and I attended the national workshop for patient service representatives in Minneapolis. What I thought when I retired, there ought to be some place where I could use the background information. I was not reluctant to get out of clinical medicine. I was not reluctant not to make any more house calls. I was not reluctant to give up the responsibility. There's a lot of other things I wanted to do. But I wanted to use my experience.

Keeping Current

Because knowledge is rapidly changing in many academic disciplines, the retired academics were asked what they needed to do to remain current in their fields after they retired. Many academics may find it more difficult to remain up-to-date in their fields after retiring, even if they try to do so, because there may be less opportunity for continued involvement in and contact with those fields. The retirees most frequently said that they tried to keep current by continuing to read the journals in their field, going to professional meetings, and continuing to interact with former students and colleagues. Retirees in the arts also mentioned the importance of attending shows and performances regularly. The following excerpts show how people from different kinds of disciplines said they tried to keep up with changing knowledge and new developments in their fields. First, two male scientists, a research university anatomy professor, aged seventy-three, and a liberal arts college astronomy professor, aged sixty-nine, talked about their efforts to keep up with the explosion of knowledge in their rapidly changing scientific specialties:

You just have to keep at it, that's all. The literature is enormous, but now there are bibliographic aids. For instance, in brain research, the Brain Research Institute at UCLA puts out periodically lists of publications, sometimes short abstracts in the various fields of brain research. They are very useful. And there are other abstract journals as well. And then the journals themselves, and nowadays nearly all the papers in the journals have abstracts at the head which you can read to see if you want to read the whole article, or else you may get enough out of it that way. But you just have to keep at it all the time. Right now, I'm trying to catch up, because I'm behind. And I go to meetings; I have gone right up to now. I'm tapering off a little on that because I have to pay my own expenses and to go to California is fairly expensive nowadays. But I go to meetings and I listen as much as I can to things I'm interested in. And what you have to do is just pick out the things you are going to really keep up on. The other stuff will float your way anyway, and you can pick it up and know whether it's important enough so that it's part of your background. It may be related to it, or else it may be the background of the whole field of neurobiology or human morphology or anything like that. I read the *American Scientist*, I read *Science*, the *New England Journal of Medicine*, which is a wonderful journal, particularly clinical, so I keep up pretty well on the clinical stuff as well as the basic.

Oh, I must. Well, I have contacts at the Houston jet propulsion lab, and anytime something happens, if it's a major session, I generally get invited to it. I hope to continue to go to the annual conventions. And then it's just a matter of reading scientific publications. There's so much material coming out that one can't keep up with all of it. But I would say that the minute I drop out of keeping current in the field, that would be the end of my contribution. I suppose I'm looked upon as the resource man in space materials for school systems within a fifty-mile radius.

Among humanities retirees, a British old civic university theologian, aged seventy-two, talked about the importance of continuing his writing, going to meetings, and keeping up with a sizable literature in his field if he was to remain current:

> Well, mainly I do quite a lot of writing in my own field. And that is something that keeps me in touch with my former colleagues here and with colleagues in other places too. I still attend conferences with fellows who are engaged in the same area of study and enjoy meeting them from time to time and sharing our ideas. It is really necessary to read the periodicals, especially periodicals where current work is reviewed, so I can find out what is being done by people and read what they say about it. One of the advantages of living in this area is access to the great library resources.

A female liberal arts college French professor, also aged seventy-two, needed to travel frequently to keep up with her field:

> I do think it is important to keep current. I was in France last summer with a retired group right in a very obscure part of France. In fact, nobody was there; no Americans were there at all. It was in the Pyrenees, on the southern part of the Mediterranean, near Spain. As I talked to the French ladies sitting in front of their houses, I'd say, "Well, I'm interested." And I would talk to them. And they always thought I was from the northern part of France, around Paris; they had never met an American and had never seen an American. And I take journals. And there is *Match* magazine, which is of course something like their *Time*, and *Express*, so when I go to the library, I get several copies of that, to keep up with it. And when I go to France, as I have done twice in the last few years, I come back with loads of books, enough to last me a few years. And there's this club at the library, so I can take my books there and turn them in and get some others. I can get a 10 percent discount as a retired teacher. I do try to keep up with my own field.

Travel was also important for keeping up-to-date in his specialty, according to a seventy-five-year-old British university retiree in civic design: "I suppose it's the usual. Read the journals to find the right books, and read the books and then travel. That's the way anyone keeps up-to-date. The traveling involves observing sights as well as going to conferences."

For artists, like this seventy-one-year-old research university painter, it was critical to continue viewing good art as well as to produce it in order to remain current:

> I like museums. I need the museums. I go to museums often. I have to have that. I have to see paintings; I have to see good ones. And the more I see of bad contemporary art, the more I need to go to a museum like the Frick or the Metropolitan to see something very good. You need stabilizing influences. And I like to see things over and over again. I mean this is a source of great pleasure, too. My favorite museum is the Frick museum. Well, that is still the greatest museum, I think; it's a small museum and everything there is a masterpiece.

Performing artists likewise needed opportunities to continue to nourish their inner artistic development. A sixty-eight-year-old liberal arts college pianist spoke eloquently of what he needed to do to continue to develop as a musician:

> Well, you need your own development primarily. You have to have open eyes to what's going on in composition and performance. But you have to look into yourself constantly to improve, not only what goes on on the outside, but your inner development which is in a constant development phase; it never stops. Every day is a new day when you go to the piano. You learn every day. I hear a great deal all the new recordings, and then I go to concerts, so that I can always compare. In me, I have an accumulation of those pianists, of those musicians who constantly help me to continue.

Finally, and not least of all, there was the need among the retired academics for the kind of human interaction that could help them remain current and involved in their fields. The retirees appreciated continued interaction with their former colleagues and students, which helped them keep abreast of what was going on in their fields and in their own departments. A research university engineer, aged seventy-six, illustrated how much continued professional and social integration — that is, a feeling of being part of things — could matter for retired academics:

One of the things I treasure is the morning coffee around here. We play a quite complex mathematical game to see who is the host. We have lots of fun and, of course, I can keep up on all the gossip. I get the ability to be in on what's going on in the college in a way I wouldn't normally. I read the literature. I've always had to do that, but now I really read it. Now, anything that comes down the road that looks interesting, I read it.

Existing without Work

"I'm trying to keep myself busy or I think I'd be miserable.

I expect to do things I have neglected in the past."

a sixty-eight-year-old male professor of music

Retirement in industrial societies is widely viewed as a fitting reward for a lifetime spent in productive labor, and older people are therefore seen as entitled to spend the bulk of their time in leisure and other nonwork pursuits. This is particularly the case as life expectancy continues to lengthen and as the time spent in active retirement grows. Retirement can be thought of as a new phase of life, one in which different activities are now appropriate. Some older people take up completely new hobbies and other leisure activities in retirement or become engaged in unpaid service activities that benefit their communities; others, in contrast, choose to spend more time in the leisure and voluntary activities they had established earlier in their lives. Such leisure and voluntary activities serve to create meaningful, functional roles for retired persons.

As is true for retirees from other occupational groups, many of the retired academics said they relished the long-awaited opportunity to spend more time on their favorite nonprofessional activities. Many expressed pleasure in being able to spend time on volunteer and leisure activities in retirement without feeling guilty that those activities competed with their professional duties. A large number of the retirees volunteered their services in unpaid activities at the local, state, or national level. At least half, both female and male, said they had participated in some kind of volunteer or service activities during their retirement. Not surprisingly, many of the unpaid volunteer activities the academics engaged in during the retirement years utilized the professional skills they had built up over a lifetime, thus providing some sense of continuity in activity patterns. For example, a retired university librarian spent hours each week reading to elementary school children, whereas a retired university physician used his professional skills in volunteering at a nursing home. The academics engaged in a great variety of leisure activities during their retirement as well as in volunteer work. The most typical leisure activities were reading, traveling, hobbies, studies outside their own professional field, walking, and watching television or listening to the radio.

In order to understand changes in leisure and service activities that occurred as a result of retirement, the academics were asked whether they had become involved in any new leisure, service, or other activities mainly since they retired. The majority responded that they had indeed taken up at least one new activity since retiring. The most frequently mentioned were various hobbies, volunteer or service activities, and work around the house or garden. Few differences were evident in the leisure and service activities of retirees from different kinds of institutions. There were some cross-national differences in activity patterns, however. For example, the British retirees were considerably more likely to be involved in gardening than were their American counterparts, probably reflecting the importance of gardening in English culture. What is more, considerably more British respondents said they had became involved in work around the house or garden mainly since they retired than did American academics, indicating a greater interest in those home-oriented activities among the British respondents. Additionally, British retirees were more likely to say that they had gotten involved in professional studies outside their own field and to have spent time on travel mainly since they retired than were their American counterparts. More traveling on the part of British academics may have reflected the smaller scale of the United Kingdom compared to the United States, as well as greater access to Europe.

Because of the almost unlimited range of choice in how to spend one's time during the retirement years, retirement may run the risk of offering too many choices and too much activity for some people. The challenge then becomes one of prioritizing activities and maintaining a reasonable activity level consistent with one's health and energy. Some of the academics had gotten so involved in numerous activities after retiring that they were confronted with the problem of running the risk of overextending themselves. This was what happened to a sixty-eight-year-old liberal arts college education professor, who described her experiences in the first year of retirement:

> My only serious problem in retirement is that I do too many things. This has really been a learning experience for me. I never realized that one could wear oneself out through pleasure just as much as through hardship. In the first year of my retirement, having no reason to say no to anything, I never did. And the result was that I had so many activities that I really ruined my health in that year of travel, and just the sort of thing that a person in my way of life would do, if they said yes to what everybody asked.

In the following pages, the retired academics describe the numerous nonprofessional activities they participated in during the retirement years. Because so many (about half) engaged in volunteer and service activities, we look first at those activities. We then turn to the main leisure activities of the retirees, including hobbies, travel, work around the home and garden, and studies outside their own professional field.

Volunteer and Service Activities

The retired academics volunteered their services in many different contexts, ranging from local community affairs to national political and environmental concerns. Many of the organizations for which they volunteered would have had difficulty keeping going economically without the efforts of those unpaid volunteers. Because the volunteer activities the academics engaged in were so varied, they are grouped into three main clusters: activities that utilized their professional skills and training or seemed related in some way to their professional lives before retirement; volunteer activities at the local, state, or national level that did not clearly utilize their professional skills; and activities in organizations involving the concerns of the demographic group to which all of the academics belonged — the elderly.

Among the many retirees who used their professional skills and training in voluntary civic-related activities were three male professors, each representing a different type of institution: an eighty-six-year-old liberal arts college economics and business administration professor, a seventy-one-year-old comprehensive university social and political sciences professor, and a sixty-eight-year-old research university education professor:

> I served a hitch on the City Council since I retired. I've been asked to fill a number of speaking dates all over the country. I've served as a mediator in labor disputes. I've had men who were in labor who were assigned as either a mediator or arbiter of an industrial situation come to me with their findings to talk over the final analysis of the situation and the setting up of a record that would be an affirmative or negative point of view.

> I was appointed by a member of the Seal Beach city council on the environmental committee down there. People are very much conscious of that. We've got such an enormous population growing out here. I was also appointed by the Board of Supervisors of Orange County to the senior citizens' council, which makes recommendations on the spending of money on senior citizens' activities in Orange County. I was on there for about two years. So I've been active in politics.

> I suppose my strong interests right now, I have two of them. One is I work for Old Capitol as a volunteer every Saturday morning. I might get more involved in that because I thoroughly enjoy it. And by the way, that is a job where I work with other guides who are work-study students. I think that one of the strongest attractions of that job for me is that I'm working with students. They are delightful to work with. They're very conscientious. We have a good

time, all of us. I really get refreshment out of that. My wife will tell you that's the one thing I never gripe about at all. I have nothing but good words for that. So she's happy to see me lead an exciting life through that job. This can perpetuate my contact with the young people.

A female liberal arts college music professor had also been engaged in civic activities, but was currently, at age eighty-three, busy utilizing her musical background to write a state history of music education:

I was on the board of Chapel View Manor. That involved, from the very beginning, from the time it was an idea, the building of housing for people above sixty-five. We built sixteen apartments under the Federal Housing Authority. Next, I happen to be state chairman of music education. I will write the state history if I live long enough.

Retirees in health fields, like this seventy-year-old British university orthopedic surgeon and seventy-year-old American research university ophthalmologist, both males, often used their professional backgrounds and skills in quite different health- and science-related settings than they had prior to their retirement:

I've been doing some half-time voluntary work at the local museum in the department of zoology, and this is relatively unskilled work with classifying, recording specimens in the collection. That's one thing I've been doing.

Hospital volunteer work is part of this business of contributing to society. So I've done quite a bit of volunteering around. One of the neglected areas of medicine, I think, are the homes, the nursing homes and places like that where doctors, lots of them, just hate to go. And a few times when I've gone, I've spent let's say half a day there or maybe even more just visiting with people. Once you get started with one room and start visiting with someone, why you go to the next one, and just visiting with people. Just someone for them to talk to outside of the families. I've been doing that in Florida.

Another health professional, a research university nurse, aged sixty-five, who was about to retire, had made plans for how she would transfer some of her skills to community service activities after retiring. She planned to do volunteer work at a university-affiliated house for families of very ill children: "Well, I have alternative plans in the back of my mind. I haven't even announced this yet, but my husband and I are very definitely interested in the Ronald McDonald house. In the potential for doing some volunteer grandparenting, or whatever."

Another woman, a seventy-eight-year-old comprehensive university speech professor, volunteered her services to the blind: "Immediately after I retired, I continued doing some work for the blind. I had read for them and taped for them when I was teaching. Then I did some newspaper reading with radio. I guess I did that about sixteen months."

Some transfer of professional interests and abilities was also evident in the volunteer activities of a British university political theorist, aged eighty-seven, who talked about his long-time political party affiliation and activities. Those activities, he added, were ones of which the interviewer "may not approve."

> I am a very active member of the Communist Party. I'm still a member of the Communist Party. I was very, very active until we moved here in 1969. When we came here, we lived further away from any branch of the Communist Party. Ever since 1919, since the end of the First World War, I've been very active in the Communist movement. I've always been active in the things I believed in. I've been very fortunate; I've been extremely healthy. I've never had anything wrong with me.

Many of the volunteer activities that the retired academics participated in did not seem to be clearly related to the professional skills and interests they had accumulated during their lives prior to retirement. Their voluntary activities simply represented a host of interests and concerns that the retirees had developed and that they now had time to focus on. A seventy-three-year-old liberal arts college English professor, for example, told of her civic activities in the political arena, as well as her work with an Area Agency on Aging since her retirement:

> Common Cause is one activity. I've been working with that since 1972 and I still am with it, partly because there isn't anybody that seems to want to work that hard. But I think that is very valuable. I was involved with the area Civil Liberties Union, with the local chapter, and then the state Civil Liberties Union. My work with the Heritage Agency on Aging meant a lot of meetings. I think it was my work with this that led into being asked to chair the committee to organize the senior center.

A sixty-five-year-old comprehensive university education professor chose to focus his volunteer activities on the fine arts and was also considering city planning:

> I've been put on the boards of two regional commissions in fine arts areas. I've always had an interest in fine arts, though that wasn't my special field of training at all. But I'm a board member of two organizations, and I've just gotten word now that they're pushing me to have membership on the town planning commission. So that may happen, and I'll probably be involved in that.

Environmental issues were the focus of a research university speech pathologist, aged sixty-five: "I've been active in the Sierra Club since 1970 and in the state chapter. Active as a lobbyist for environmental issues."

Other academics chose to volunteer in health-care settings. An eighty-nine-year-old professor of French and Italian described her work as a Gray Lady, which ended only when her own health eventually became problematic:

> One thing, when I retired I went into Gray Lady work. And I'd always wanted to do that and never had time to do Gray Lady work. I enjoyed that very much and would have liked to keep on with it, but I got this inner ear difficulty. I read mostly or talked to people or sometimes helped them with their meals. I happened to be in the dermatology department and many of them had diseased

hands and things like that and couldn't do things. But often it was just a matter of sitting and talking with them, listening to them talk about their families and things of that sort. But I did read a lot to them, and I wrote letters for them, and things of that sort. I just loved it. I had a card this Christmas from one of the patients there twenty years ago; he was a young man at that time, maybe twenty or twenty-five years old.

A number of the retired academics became heavily involved in church-related or church-sponsored volunteer activities. Two male retirees, a seventy-year-old research university radiology professor and a seventy-six-year-old comprehensive university foreign languages professor, talked about their church-related work:

I just was elected president of the local Gideon Society or group. I have been treasurer this year and nobody else was willing, so I was elected president. This is going to take some time. All the details, organization, and planning meetings, and so on. I will be retiring from the section of the church at the same time, so I won't continue that, but I may continue to serve on the adult education committee at the church. It's a subcommittee of the Christian education committee, and our responsibility is to plan all of the adult education programs.

Well, I belong to a church which has a program which is called the Cross program. The word "cross" is an acronym for something which I can't remember. But it has a clergyman whose job is to spend full-time on this program. Now, one of the things he does is to find people who are in trouble, people who need this, that, or the other assistance. For example, there may be in the church bulletin a little notice that says there is a woman who needs a ride to Toledo to visit her son who is in an institution there. And I told him right away I would take her. I've taken a woman to university hospital whose husband was dying in the hospital. I provided transportation every day except one in the week for a small boy who went to a nursery school at the Methodist church. He would be brought there by a school bus at about noon, and then he would spend the afternoon in this nursery school. But somebody had to bring him home, and I went four days a week and brought him home. This program constantly utilizes the volunteer assistance of people in the church and other people who are not in our church. So I've done quite a little volunteer work in connection with that.

A British university pediatrician, aged sixty-eight, was likewise quite heavily involved in activities of his church:

I do quite a lot of church work. I don't know if you know about this sort of setup, about the lay ministry in the church. The people who are called "lay readers"—this is the Anglican Church, the Church of England—they take part in the services. They help and that sort of thing, and other activities in the parish. And I've been doing that for forty years. Since retiring, I of course have an opportunity to take an even greater part in this. And various opportunities arise.

Some retirees, like this seventy-eight-year-old British woman from the faculty of education, also played active roles in local historical or political organizations after retiring:

I am president of the historical association, of the local branch. It is run by my old students. I don't do much for it, but they come to me and we discuss it; we're the committee, as it were. We run it and we have done some very successful things. Also, in recent years, I've been taking a more active part in the local Liberal associations. I'm on various committees for that, more than I like, really. But I meet a lot of people that way, and we organize things of various kinds. Again, it's a case of I'm not now able to be very active and go around as much as I did, so other people have to do the running around, but I've got a telephone. So I can work through the telephone, so we can discuss things. I don't think I was active in the Liberals before retirement; I think that came afterwards. Because when I was teaching, I didn't really have time to do that sort of thing.

Although there was not widespread involvement with seniors' organizations on the part of these academic retirees, some did attend senior centers or other organizations oriented primarily to the concerns of older persons. More frequently, however, the retirees volunteered their services to organizations serving the elderly. The following comments by two male retirees, a research university engineering professor, aged sixty-six, and a comprehensive university English professor, aged seventy-four, illustrate their roles as both volunteers and consumers at senior centers. Their time investment in senior center activities, especially for the second man, was considerable.

Yes, I'm connected with the Senior Center and director of Meals on Wheels one day a week. I'm in the chorus for the Senior Center. My wife and I started in every day on slow aerobics class. But it's only twice a week, and so we decided to take the ideas and do it at home. So we do twenty-five minutes of slow aerobics at home every day.

I deliver meals five days a week. This takes up about three hours a day. But I tell the people if they need anything on Saturday or Sunday to give me a call. I average about twenty-two or twenty-three meals a day, sometimes twenty-seven or twenty-eight. Well, I have the longest route now. I delivered twenty-two meals this morning. Normally I don't spend much time with them if they don't need anything. I have a couple in there in their nineties who are almost completely blind and almost completely deaf. They depend on me to read their letters to them, write checks for them. I've taken them down to get their taxes reduced on the house. I've taken one down to settle the matter of an estate and will of a relative which he was executing. I've taken them to the doctor and I've gone to the veterans' hospital to pick up medicine for them and things like that. A good many of them tell me their life stories.

Working with older people appeared to help some retirees better understand and deal with their own aging. According to a seventy-one-year-old research university nurse, serving as a volunteer for several organizations that were devoted to the concerns of the aging and the aged helped her cope with her own aging process:

I have gotten into the Council on Aging, and this is more social work than it is nursing. So I have had quite a little bit of contact with students in social work. There was a course in counseling, where the instructor had his students visit for a semester once a week with elderly people, and this I enjoyed tremendously. When I took my master's, I was forced to work with older people, and I found that I wasn't adjusting to it very well. My emotional response to older people was less than desirable. So, to help cope with my own aging, I felt that I had to do something. And the way to do this was to get out and work with them and to get to know them better. I've been involved in the American Association of Retired Persons. That's another organization that is a lobbying group. I've been working with that.

Leisure Activities

The leisure activities the retired academics were involved in do not fall easily into discrete conceptual categories. Like most other retirees, these academic retirees engaged in a host of hobbies, ranging from painting and music to spectator and active sports. Many, especially the men, spent more time than they had prior to retirement in home-related projects, including home repair and housework, and in work around the yard or garden. Not surprisingly for retired academics, a large majority traveled during their retirement and engaged in considerable amounts of leisure reading. What is more, about half of the academics pursued an area of study outside their own professional field after retiring; their intellectual interests included such fields as art, foreign languages, archaeology, photography, and genealogy.

Hobbies

Among favorite hobbies pursued by the retirees, arts and crafts activities were fairly common. Indeed, for a few retirees, their hobby developed into a full-time vocation. A sixty-four-year-old research university pediatrician, for instance, spent every day from nine until four working on cabinetry in a local woodworking shop, an activity he thoroughly enjoyed. Some retirees who worked with their hands in their former occupation, like this male British university orthopedic surgeon, aged seventy, learned to use their hands in quite new ways after retiring: "I've taken up what I was always interested in doing, various handicrafts like tapestry work and embroidery work and painting, which I've always been interested in but never had time to do. There wasn't time."

Some retirees concentrated on painting after retiring. Two British men, one a seventy-one-year-old from the faculty of education and the other a sixty-eight-year-old physiologist, spoke of their new artistic interest with obvious enthusiasm:

> The only thing I've taken up since retirement is a class in painting. I joined a class in painting about two or three years ago. Something I've been promising myself to do when I retire anyhow. I'm interested in looking at paintings. I wanted to do it for my own interest and amusement. I like sketching also.

> I've gotten sort of interested in painting. This is a new interest. I never did it before. It takes up a lot of my time. I went to a course, also. I like to spend my time in this way. What I'm doing now is entirely different than what I was doing before.

Music was a favorite hobby for a number of retirees. According to two male research university retirees in their early seventies, a French and secondary education professor and a library science professor, retirement offered much more time to devote to their long-term musical interests:

> I suppose that my experience is unique. As a youth in New Orleans I played tenor banjo and sang in local dance bands, even while in high school. This skill permitted me to earn my way through college and university until I came to this university in 1935. Now that we have retired and live in Hawaii, I have joined the Hawaii international ukulele club. I have a specially made instrument that can be played much as a classical guitar. Have a full life! Even appear in concerts with the club.

> I have a hobby that is rather extraordinary. I have been an Italian opera fan for years, particularly a lover of Verdi's operas. And everybody who knows music at all knows four or five of Verdi's operas. He wrote twenty-seven. And who knows the other twenty-three? Hardly anybody does. So a couple of years before I retired, I

started to collect albums of Verdi's operas and got myself a good stereo equipment set. And so now in an odd afternoon that I don't feel like reading, I listen to a Verdi opera. And I bought these one at a time, maybe one a month or so, not that often. You have to listen to them at the time to make sure the record isn't defective. But now that I got through all that and I'm retired, I started with this first opera and went through them. And now I'm going through them for the second time. Now I may listen to one a week, or one every other week, or twice a week. And this has been a most interesting thing to do. It's similar to reading Shakespeare. Each opera or play is an independent creation. It's that kind of activity that you have time for.

British retirees also were pleased to have more time to spend on music. A computer scientist, aged sixty-two, talked about spending more time on his piano: "I've taken up music quite strongly. I play the piano; not very well. I just play well enough for my own amusement. I play a lot more now than before retirement."

Artistic expression was manifested for some retirees in creative writing. This liberal arts college music professor, aged seventy-two, returned to an interest in writing she had developed long before her retirement:

Well, I was not a music major in college; I was an English major. And so it's kind of fun to be doing a little writing now. I've had a couple of editorials in the paper, and I correspond with people who have a literary bent, and we pool our resources, happily. These are requested editorials. It's nonfiction.

For some of the male retirees, cooking became a new form of expression during the retirement years. Indeed, a few were serious enough about this activity to sign up for regular classes. A British university psychologist, aged seventy-five, told about his culinary achievements: "I went to classes for cooking. I now know how to cook much better. I like to do basic cooking really—sweets, pastries, vegetables, and things like that. I went to class for a year, once a week."

Another man, a research university professor of education and theater arts, aged sixty-six, likewise described his culinary accomplishments:

> Cooking. I may as well tell you about that. It's been coming on for a couple of years, and with the freedom of retirement, Barbara doesn't have much chance to do cooking anymore. But she doesn't complain. It just opened up a new area. Just experimenting in all the ethnic groups. I'll often sit down and work out the week's menu in advance.

Another activity that was of interest to the retirees, as it is for many older people, was keeping as physically fit as possible. Some of the academics were involved in a variety of sports activities in order to remain physically fit, a few even until advanced ages. This healthy ninety-one-year-old British chemist, for example, described his enjoyment of cycling and mountaineering in retirement:

> For forty years, anyhow, I was a cyclist. I cycled all over England, Scotland, Wales, Ireland. My wife said, "If you buy another new bicycle, I shall leave you." I was threatening to buy a new one at seventy-five. When I retired, I got some spare time in which I could do some exploring that I hadn't done before. I also did some mountain-climbing, both here and in Switzerland, and in Austria.

His colleague from physical education, aged seventy-one, described his own unusual physical activity:

> Sailing on the canals. Since retirement I've had the time to develop it. There are all kinds of organizations or associations. For a long time the canals were neglected and were nearly lost, and this is an association that has been formed to recover them. It's a national organization and this is one of our late interests, the restoration of canals. I was asked to be on the local committee before I retired. We began to find the canals then. And then afterwards I was able to devote more time to it. There are United States associations. I have met up with a lot of Americans on the canals. Not so many as last year; this year there has been a large number of Scandinavians. As well as seeing the canals, you get to see the country as well.

Yoga was a way of keeping fit for a sixty-eight-year-old liberal arts college musician:

I do a lot of yoga and I teach yoga. And I teach more yoga than before. The physical part. And I love to teach yoga. I like to work with the human body, to see an improvement in the whole state. Actually, I started it in Paris. I always wanted to do something which does not involve group work. My yoga teacher was an Indian who had a studio. I worked with him for a year and a half, and then later he let me work with newcomers.

More commonly, however, the retirees tended to engage in sports like golf. This sport was enjoyed by a research university professor of education and theater arts who also mentioned taking up cooking in his mid-sixties. He spoke of playing golf and of other physical activities during the months he spent in the southern United States:

Yeah, we're both starting to play golf again. We haven't played for fifteen to twenty years. Played quite a bit down South. Got a little hooked on pine boat surf and pier fishing down South. It's just a whole new area that sort of opened up and I'm sure we'll pursue it more next winter. Last year just from ads we picked a little place on the Gulf shores of Alabama. It was very nice.

A few additional excerpts from the tapes illustrate the wide variety of interesting hobbies the retirees said they enjoyed during their retirement, including birdwatching and wildlife conservation (by a seventy-one-year-old female British veterinarian), stamp collecting (by an eighty-six-year-old American male comprehensive university physicist), and photography and indoor gardening under fluorescent lights (by a seventy-two-year-old liberal arts college English professor):

Birdwatching, perhaps a bit more. I've attended ornithology classes, evening classes, and so on. I'm interested in birdwatching. I decided if I were to do something in the locality the thing that would offend me least was probably getting mixed up with the local World Wildlife group, and I'm currently chairman of that. It's a very small group; they're essentially fundraising. But the attitude toward fundraising in this group is that we don't want to just shake tins under people's noses and hold out hands for money; we want to give them something in return, so we put on two or three lectures a year from good speakers.

Well, there was something immediately after I retired. I was a member of the men's stamp club here in town. They elected me secretary-treasurer. I spent quite a good deal of my time in that immediately after retirement. It was something new.

I had spent three years in China, from 1931 to 1934. I wanted to have a record of it. I made trips back into the interior and I took an awful lot of photographs. I even had one article accepted for *National Geographic.* They never published it; they don't publish a tenth of what they buy. I took a trip down the river to Guilin to a place where the three rivers come together. I took pictures of these mountains and I took pictures also of the people. When I got back, I got interested in color photography. And I thought I'd like to have a studio. I ran this studio for about two years, from 1973 to 1975. One thing that is new is growing my own plants in the basement under fluorescent lights, so that when the last frost is over I have big, healthy plants. This year I grew forty-eight tomato plants. Impatiens, petunias, snapdragons, coleus, shasta daisies, eggplant, broccoli. I'm trying to expand this into some sort of a hothouse attached to a window, so that it can be heated from the heat of the house, and have double panes so I can have serious growing. The interest in gardening goes way back, but this is new.

Travel

About three-quarters of the retirees said that one of their retirement activities was traveling. Although some of them had traveled extensively for their work prior to retirement, others said that they had been able to travel little because of their work obligations. Now all had the freedom to travel, in a very leisurely way if they wished, to destinations that were attractive to them. A British university retiree in civic design, aged seventy-five, for example, wanted to go to far-away countries he had not had the opportunity to visit. He said simply: "I hadn't visited South Africa or New Zealand before I retired."

Many of the very recent retirees in particular marveled at the new travel possibilities open to them. Illustrating this newfound ability to travel more were two American male professors in the transition to retirement study, a professor of medicine, aged sixty-three, and a professor of education, aged seventy, who talked about their extensive travels during their first year of retirement:

> For the first time, I've been able to travel considerably. I was able to visit two daughters in Colorado last fall. And this spring I've just returned from a five-and-a-half week European vacation, which is far longer than any vacation I've ever had totally in a year or so. We have two daughters in France, so we visited them. And then we went through Italy and Greece, and then back through Austria and Germany, where I have a nephew, and back to France. We were with a daughter there another couple of weeks. We had a very delightful time.

> I particularly like the freedom to go places and do things at times when I want to. For instance, we made a trip out West and seeing Yosemite without crowds of people was great. Whereas if I had had to go in July and August, it would have been terrible with people. So I've enjoyed that very much. Since our retirement, we've made one trip out to the Northwest, one trip to Texas, and one trip out to California and back. We can't keep that pace up, but that's been great. And one trip to the East Coast. So that's been a major occupation.

This is not to say that people who had been retired for longer periods did not relish the opportunity to travel more. An eighty-nine-year-old research university professor of French and Italian, for example, was delighted with her chance to travel:

> There was a lot of traveling that I wanted to do and never had time. And since I retired, my brother and I have traveled quite a lot, just around the United States, not out of the States. Retirement gives you the freedom to do many things which you have not been able to do before.

And her male colleague, aged seventy-two, from the department of mechanics and hydraulics, communicated his sense of liberation about now being able to travel extensively:

> In our case, we'd never traveled a whole lot, because we'd have the two weeks at Christmas-time and two weeks in August. Getting a month during the year. My appointment was eleven months. So we did the usual things; we'd go somewhere for Christmas, our parents' home, or we'd go fishing in the fall, or take a short trip around here. But we never got further than Canada or Mexico. So we really started seeing some of the things I always had a hankering to see. We've made one or two major trips every year. This has been a lot of fun.

For some academics, retirement meant the opportunity to take trips to places where they had spent a period earlier in their lives. Now that they were free of their professional duties, they had time to return to those places. A British university psychologist, aged seventy-five, returned with his wife to visit the country where they had lived for a number of years: "We've been to two trips to New Zealand since I retired. My wife is an Australian, so we had long connections there. We went out to New Zealand in 1938 and I was there all through the war. I only intended to be there for three years, but then the war started."

The overwhelming impression conveyed was that there was now time for traveling at a really leisurely pace, without the schedules and time constraints imposed by work. Medical retirees in particular, who had often been tied to a very tight schedule, expressed much pleasure in having new time available for travel. Two male physicians, a seventy-three-year-old American research university ophthalmologist and a sixty-eight-year-old British old civic university pediatrician, described all the traveling they were now doing:

> We have enjoyed travel, I'm telling you, because we're not in any hurry to get anyplace. We drove to Seattle and back this year. We went to Alaska. And if you can do these kinds of things, travel, while it's becoming a little more expensive, is very, very exciting, and visiting people — friends, relatives, whatever you wish — we've

really had a great time doing that. Now, for example, sometimes we'll drive as far as, oh, five hundred miles in a day, and the next day, we may only drive a hundred miles or even less. If you want to stay, if you want to stop off some place, it's the way you want it. The only thing that keeps you from it is your budget.

One was on duty, day and night, so to speak, more or less the whole year. In a clinical department, you don't get the sort of leave that the nonclinical departments get. The terms don't apply, because we had students coming all through, including the patients. I enjoy the opportunities of traveling around, which we didn't have before. For example, my wife and I have been to Kenya, we've been to Cyprus, we've been to the Canary Islands, as well as traveling around in European countries like Norway, and so on, which we've always liked to do. So that the opportunity of doing this, not confined to a particular time when you can get off from your duties, has been good. For instance, we decided last week that perhaps it might be a good idea to have a break, and we've arranged a touring holiday by car going through South Wales and around there, you see. Now, this was all arranged within a couple of days. You couldn't do that sort of thing before. We always liked to travel, and we've had opportunities, rather limited ones. But now we can.

Work around the Home or Garden

Home-based activities like fix-up projects around the house or work in the yard or garden were also popular among the retirees. Often these projects were ones that had been delayed considerably because the academics simply had little free time to devote to such activities prior to retirement. Consequently, at least in the early years, retirement offered a catch-up time for home-based activities for many. These activities were what made retirement pleasurable, according to an eighty-one-year-old research university music professor: "Yard work, gardening, all those things are what make retirement satisfying; because you have time to do these things." As mentioned previously, gardening was more popular among the British than the American academics. The following comments by a British psychologist, aged seventy-four, and her male colleague, a seventy-seven-year-old dentist, reflect this interest:

> I think the main one is gardening. I began it before I retired. You've got to remember our department specialized in the psychology of aging and retirement. We were well prepared. I began the gardening. In fact, I built this house and came here to live, knowing that I was going to stay until I retired. And I was going to garden.

> Of necessity, gardening. I do all of my own gardening. One thing you've got to do is keep at it. It doesn't take my whole thoughts. I want to have it as my outside interest. I want to be able to go away and not have to worry about it. It's a good thing at times, this gardening, and it can be interesting.

Some academics engaged in larger-scale agricultural endeavors. A British university retiree, aged eighty, from the department of Italian studies, wrote of her activities on her property in Italy: "Much work in my Italian house and grounds, which I acquired one year before retirement and where I live about five months a year. There are many new activities connected with my new home in Tuscany—fruit farming, wine-making, harvesting."

A few American academics also took on large-scale agricultural projects. A research university religion professor, aged sixty-five, who was about to retire, said he had planned ahead for such activities in retirement: "I already own forty acres in the country and I plan to continue to plant trees and things like that." Two men who had already retired from the same university, a mathematics professor, aged seventy-two, and an education professor, aged seventy-four, both moved to Minnesota farms, where they started major projects:

> We don't raise anything anymore on this place. At one time this was a hundred and eighty acres. But my brother retired ten years ago, and when he retired he had to dispose of some cattle and equipment that was on the farm here. And we sold a hundred and sixty acres of the farm, so there's only, oh, it's only some eighteen acres now. And when I came home here, we still had about ten acres on the place that had been in field. And we decided then that

we'd take this field and put it back into trees. So I got some help here from the Department of Natural Resources, and I got trees, and I had trees planted on the place. And I got a watering system, so I keep them going. I've got about twelve acres now that I've planted with trees since I came home. It's over fifteen hundred trees all together. I've got equipment so that I can work with them, and that's really what it takes. If you were going to do it all by hand, it would be a frightful chore. So I've got about two hundred green ashes, and I've got about one hundred, I believe, of the hackberries, and I've got two hundred of the oaks, and I've got two hundred of the black walnuts, and then I've got some evergreens on the place here. That takes care of most of it.

We live in a community up here that's under a great deal of pressure for development. We're only twenty miles out of the cities, and we're in what might be referred to as a metropolitan area. Yet we are rural. We live on a farm ourselves here, and there are farms around us. On our farm here we have opportunities to do things. I started a new apple orchard. And my wife thinks that I have holes in my head for starting an apple orchard at this age. But I did it largely because on our farm here there are some old, old orchards that were dying, and I wanted to propagate those in the form of new trees. I wanted to preserve them, I should say. Of course, you do that by grafting into new stock and starting new trees.

With regard to work around the house itself, most retirees were committed to staying in their present homes and therefore put considerable effort into taking care of them. Sometimes the maintenance problems, especially in older homes, were substantial. This did not faze a research university music professor, aged eighty-one, who was still doing all of his own home repairs — and who presented a list of his activities to prove it!

My other interests (besides music) are pretty largely physical. For instance, home repair. We've got property here. I do all the electrical, plumbing, carpentry, brickwork, cement work. I do all the upkeep on the property, you see. That's what I meant earlier when I said people should develop before they retire some skills and interests outside their regular profession.

A British university retiree, aged seventy-eight, from the faculty of education, described her efforts in trying to keep her home in good repair:

> I could have left this house. But I decided not to do that. It takes quite a lot of energy and quite a lot of time running a house this size. There are five other people living in it. And it's my house, so that I'm in charge of it, so I get to organize it. That takes quite a lot of time. When I was in hospital, I think that the other people in the house were really surprised at the amount of time that I would have spent on it, because a fridge broke down and something else went wrong, and one person came and said, "If the roof comes off, I retire." There were many things going wrong that they had to deal with; normally, I deal with those things. I organize the people who work here; there's a boy doing the garden now. The house is definitely an interest, you know, and also there are people in it. I'm not by myself. We are always reconstructing the garden or doing something to it. It can look very beautiful in the summer, but it's still got a lot of things needing to be done with it.

Caring for a home or garden could involve significant role reversals on the part of couples, usually when spouses became too ill or frail to manage the home responsibilities that formerly had been theirs. A British university chemist, aged eighty-three, described how versatile he had become in homemaking tasks: "You've got to be adaptable around the house without worrying about it. Especially if your wife has an illness or breaks a bone, you've got to be able to help her out. I'm a reasonable cook, and I help my wife if she needs it in any area."

Likewise, a newly retired research university dean, aged sixty-nine, and his colleague in education, aged sixty-six, talked about helping their sick wives during the first year of their retirement. The first man referred to himself as a "homemaker."

> My wife's health is not so good, and that has been an increasing problem. I probably spend more time with her, and keeping the house up, and things of that sort than time I spend at the office. I work more and more at home.

Another thing that keeps me busy is that, because my wife is not well, I do virtually all the cooking. I don't object to it. I clean; I do more cleaning. There is one I don't like; I don't like to clean up after a meal.

Studies outside One's Professional Field

Not surprisingly for people who had spent their lives in intellectual pursuits, almost all of the retired academics engaged in a substantial amount of leisure reading during retirement. Their enjoyment of reading in areas unrelated to their professional work was exemplified by a male research university German professor, aged seventy-three: "From my point of view, I can now read everything that I want to read, rather than having to read, you know, for professional purposes. There is no compulsion." Interestingly, about half of the retirees had focused their reading and intellectual interests on studying one or more subject areas outside their own professional field. These interests seemed to bear no clear relation to their former professional lives. Sometimes their studies reflected long-term interests; at other times, they were interests that had developed during retirement. Some of the retirees attended formal classes; others, however, chose to undertake an informal program of self-learning. The topics they studied were quite varied and included music, history, archaeology, philosophy, theology, and genealogy. Among those taking formal classes were two education retirees, a sixty-seven-year-old male from the American comprehensive university and a seventy-seven-year-old female from a British old civic university, and her colleague, a seventy-two-year-old male pathologist:

I'm involved in taking classes at a community college here [in Oregon] that offers courses for senior citizens as well as for other people, and so I decided to go back to school. So I've been enjoying that; just sitting in classes and taking work. I'm studying music, believe it or not!

Many people do what I did, that is, attend extramural classes in whatever subject interests you. I think that's stimulating. I think a change of interest or a change of subject is very challenging. Because I think a problem, I would say, about retirement is the lack of challenge. All of the challenges go, and I would think to create new ones for yourself is quite a good thing. I want to learn, not to teach. I've involved myself in philosophy and theology, where I was a newcomer, a complete newcomer. And that really meant attending lectures and learning. Quite definitely you are a pupil, you see. I involved myself in the extramural courses that were linked to the theology in the Cathedral, and that of course meant not only attending, but perhaps taking a more active part in debate or activities that involves a weekend studying something. And I have been doing that quite consistently for the last four years. I intend to receive information. I think it's lovely; it's fascinating, really. And I think you can actually give a good deal in being an interested pupil, you see. Very often in discussion and debate, one can contribute a lot.

I take a bit more interest in local history. Since I have retired I have taken evening classes. It's been very interesting because they're all retired people. This is an interesting polytechnic, rather popular course. They go around with a tape-recorder and find out what people did in about 1900. And I have an interest in archaeology.

Other academics who were planning to retire soon had made plans for classes they would take after retiring, like this American research university surgeon, aged seventy, who discussed his keen interest in astronomy:

I'm very interested in astronomy. Messing around with that quite a bit. I haven't done very much yet because I'm still working and I don't have time. When I have time I'm going to get a telescope, go take some classes at the College of the Desert. I've previously taken courses in astronomy, so I know a little about it. I've read a lot of stuff.

Not all of the formal learning situations that the retirees took part in involved studying academic subjects. Instead, some of the classes that interested them dealt with practical topics that related to their daily lives. A sixty-eight-year-old British woman from the faculty of education, for example, described weekend courses she attended that were designed for people who wanted to learn more about gardening:

I mentioned to you gardeners' weekends. This links up with having more time. I've always liked growing things, and getting nice borders and things. Just before we retired, I happened to catch sight of an advertisement in the *Observer* on a Sunday: Gardeners' Weekends, a firm in Haddersfield. And they had a host and hostess. The host was Robert St. John. And we booked for this. They are run by a travel firm. You go up on the Friday to somewhere. And because we went by public transport, we were collected at the station and taken to a reasonably good hotel usually—always, really. You met the other people, all of whom were interested in gardens in some way, either in keeping them or going to see them. In the evening, the host would give a talk on some aspect of gardening. The Saturday, off you went in a coach, because they never took more than forty if they could help it. You went to see a garden, had lunch somewhere, went to see another garden. And because of Robert St. John, you always got the top people at these institutes. That evening, you would have an outside speaker after dinner. The Sunday, two more places, and then tea time around about five or half-past five. That was the end of the weekend.

Other academics chose to study the topics that interested them on their own. Illustrative are a male British university engineer, aged seventy-one, a female American liberal arts college mathematician, aged seventy-nine, and a male American research university dental pathologist, aged seventy-two, who talked about their respective studies of history, theology, and archaeology. His expertise in archaeology led to unpaid work for the dental pathologist.

I took up history when I retired, or actually just before I retired. Six years ago. I am filled with admiration for historians, as a matter of fact. I never realized how much legwork there is. I am trying to find the house that Whitworth's first wife died in. It sounds dark, but that's what I'm trying to do. It probably took me six months to find it. It's in Cheshire, not far from Chester.

My church work is mainly with a women's group. In our church, we have had our women divided into groups, into circles, as we call it. And we presented study work to the circles. And I have done that in my own circle, and sometimes in other circles. In our book group, this past year it was a series of studies in *Concern* magazine on the festivals of the church.

I've been interested most of my adult life in the field of archaeology and physical anthropology. I gave it up in the 1940s as a profession because of the economic circumstances of the country. And while my interest continued, I had to delay getting back to work in that field until after I retired. I'm helping out the local archaeological programs as I can. I'm working with the office of the state archaeologist part-time on a gratuitous basis, and I've been teaching a course in the anthropology department for the past two years, also on a gratuitous basis. I've enjoyed every moment of it. I think that's one of the strongest substitutes for my routine employment prior to retirement. I have a lot of subsidiary interests. But they're not at all dominant. All science interests me. Astronomy especially, largely because my wife's interested in astronomy too. We have our own portable observatory.

Lastly, and not uncommonly among older people, a few of the retired academics developed an interest in genealogy. These two men, an American research university musician, aged eighty-one, and a British old civic university psychologist, aged seventy-five, shared a serious interest in tracking down their family histories:

I've also done some writing or research on my genealogy. For about three years, I've gone extensively into that. I've made a rather serious study of it and printed a good size book on that.

I got interested in family history, and I decided I'm going to find out about my ancestors. So I took a class in genealogy. And looking up family records in archives, and things of that kind.

Summing Up

Nearly two decades ago, I set out to try to understand as best I could the experiences of professors in retirement. These, I thought, were a rather unusual group of people, an occupational group so committed to their professional work that they retired several years later than did most other people and very commonly continued their professional activities well into the retirement years. What was it that kept them going, sometimes even until very advanced ages? Alternatively, what was it that caused some of them to ease out of or even completely drop their professional involvements once retired?

What impressed me most then and still does today is the enormous variety of human experience that I encountered in my years of interviewing. I received a multitude of impressions in those years, sometimes conflicting, as I talked with men and women from different institutions, different disciplines, whose ages spanned nearly half a century: of the many who were happy in retirement and of some who were sad; of those who accepted their retired status and those who were embittered by it; of those who seemed vitally involved in professional or nonprofessional pursuits and others who suffered from ennui and lack of direction; of those who praised their institution and colleagues for not forgetting them and those who railed against those institutions and colleagues for forgetting them. Consequently, there were many retirements for me to study. Yet, despite this diversity, there were also the regularities, the themes, the common patterns that emerged from the more than four hundred interviews that were conducted, so that we can get a sense of the commonality as well as the uniqueness of the academic retirement experience. Without, I believe, their being led in any purposeful way, the retired academics made some common points over and over again, told of experiences that occurred time and again, and expressed often similar feelings. In attempting to categorize and generalize about the thoughts and reactions the academics shared with me, I have tried to be as true as possible to their comments and to convey the sense of what they were trying so eloquently to express about their lives in retirement. I have also tried to disentangle as much as possible the retirement experience from other age-related changes that were occurring simultaneously in their lives, in particular declining health and bereavement. Those normative changes that accompany later life cannot but have an impact on retirement, and I do not mean to minimize them; but at the same time, those processes and events of later life should not be confused with the effects of retirement itself.

Themes and Patterns

Adaptation

"I didn't notice any psychological depression. I didn't anticipate it with any great horror. And when it came, I accepted it without any feeling of being let down or anything. The sun still shone." This seventy-four-year-old professor of German communicated the feelings of the majority of his colleagues about retirement: the sun did indeed still continue to rise each morning for most of these retired academic men and women. Despite their loss of a central and often cherished life role, despite their feeling sometimes quite separated from their institutions, the lives of these academics did not end with retirement. Quite the contrary. Most of the retirees communicated a spirit of resilience and adaptability in dealing with their retired status, an ability to deal, sooner or later, with a major life transition that meant their formal separation from the world of work. The academics all knew that retirement was coming; indeed, that it was inevitable. (Recall that all of the interviews occurred before the end of mandatory retirement in American academe in 1994.) Most of the academics, in both the United States and the United Kingdom, accepted retirement as a normal, and predictable, phase of their lives and had made some sort of peace with it. In fact, the majority (but certainly not all) looked forward to retirement and planned for it to some degree — a sort of anticipation of the future that may have helped hasten their adaptation. And when retirement did come, virtually all of the academics — across institutions, nation, gender, age, and discipline — had positive things to say about their retired status. Generally, the academics were far more positive than negative about retirement. What they appreciated in the retirement phase of their lives were the things that most people hope for throughout their lives, but may not have the opportunity to experience freely until later in life: freedom from various burdens and schedules and time to spend exactly as one wishes. For many of the academics, retirement offered a better balance of the nonprofessional and professional parts of their lives than they had previously enjoyed; and although most continued to work at some aspects of their life profession, they could now do so on their own time, at their own pace, and without the numerous institutional and departmental constraints and demands of their earlier lives. Even some academics who had initially resisted retirement discovered that it offered some pleasant surprises and eventually came to at least accept, if not to enjoy, their retired status.

The downside of all this, however, was that more than half of the retirees also identified negative aspects of their retirement. For a few, the situation was bleak; they were the people who felt that they were completely put out to pasture, formally separated from their institutions, their colleagues, and, most importantly, their work. Those academics expressed feelings ranging from sadness to anger to bitterness, and often eloquently so. They were inconsolable, sometimes even after many years of retirement. More commonly, however, although the academics identified some aspects of retirement that they did not like, including loss of status after retiring, loss of facilities, and, most frequently, loss of the intellectual and professional stimulation of like-minded students and colleagues who had for decades been a given in their lives, they did not view retirement as a mainly negative experience. Whether this was simply an acceptance of what they could not change is hard to say.

Although retirement, like all life course changes, is an experience from which people must ultimately learn firsthand, they can be informed by others who have already experienced this new phase of life. When the retired academics were asked what advice they would offer to others who were soon to retire, they spoke in a rather consistent voice about what they thought had helped them adapt to retirement and would therefore be useful for others: most importantly, that people should plan ahead for their retirement, so that they do not go into it blindly, and that, once retired, people should stay as active as their health and energy permitted. Drawing from their own experience, they also had suggestions for their various institutions to deal more effectively and humanely with younger academics who were approaching retirement age. Those suggestions ranged from changes that would be relatively simple to implement, such as clarifying their emeritus status and providing reduced fees for parking and campus events, to a more systematic approach of informing faculty about financial benefits in retirement and providing more facilities for them to continue their professional work after formally retiring. A common thread that ran through their comments was a strong desire to remain connected in some way to the institutions that they had long served and felt part of—not to be cut off and perhaps even alienated from them. Such feelings of continued inclusion, not exclusion, are important in facilitating older persons' feelings of well-being and continued social integration.

Continuity

"A wise person has said that the best preparation for tomorrow is to live well today. We carry into retirement essentially the same kind of person we were before retirement. If we have tried to live as best we can physically, mentally, and spiritually before retirement, then when retirement comes, we shall go on trying to mold ourselves into the kind of persons we ought to be. And if we have learned something of the secrets of happiness before retirement, these will serve us well after we retire." Many retirees, like this seventy-six-year-old male liberal arts college professor of religion and philosophy, expressed their belief in the importance of continuing lifelong patterns of behavior in the retirement years. The theme of continuity, of retaining valued lifelong patterns of thought and action as much as possible, ran through the interviews. Gerontologists know that, although both continuity and change characterize later life, it appears that older people try to maintain basic patterns of personality and activity as much as is feasible and comfortable.

For many of the retirees, the secret of happiness in retirement was professional role continuity: continuing as best they could favorite aspects of their professional life before retirement. Four out of five of these academic retirees continued some kind of professional work during their retirement: they continued to teach when possible; they did research; they created artworks, musical compositions, and poetry and prose; they consulted; they kept current by going to professional meetings and reading journals and books in their fields. In fact, retirees sometimes saw retirement as the opportunity for a new life in which they could really focus on what they liked to do professionally; indeed, some said they had retired to work. This continuity of work activity extended even to some very old retirees. Thus, we saw the ninety-one-year-old British chemist who continued to teach until he was eighty-four, the ninety-six-year-old American research university English professor who continued his work on Chaucer and Shakespeare from his nursing home bed ("It is art for art's sake; I did some this morning"), and the eighty-six-year-old liberal arts college musician who continued to give her music lessons in New York City. At younger ages, there were even more academics who remained professionally active. As Mark H. Ingraham, himself a retired professor and dean emeritus of arts and sciences at the University of Wisconsin, pointed out several decades ago, their purpose held (*My Purpose Holds: Reactions and Experiences in Retirement of TIAA-CREF Annuitants*). Why it held, I would venture from the interviews, had to do with the academics' lifelong interest in, and commitment to, a field of inquiry which they found very absorbing. This intellectual interest and commitment patterned their lives.

With regard to continuity of life patterns, we were interested in knowing whether or not the same factors that contributed to satisfaction prior to retirement also contributed to satisfaction after retirement. To examine this question, we looked at various work and non-work activity patterns of the academics prior to and in retirement, as well as important personal characteristics that might affect their satisfaction, including self-perceived health, financial status, sex, marital status, and length of retirement. We discovered that some professional role orientations and activity patterns were associated with satisfaction among the academics, whereas others were not. Most notably, involvement in academic administration seemed unrelated to satisfaction of the academics either prior to or after retirement, whereas other professional roles such as teaching, research, and consulting were associated with pre- and postretirement satisfaction. Additionally, personal factors such as good health and adequate finances were strongly associated with satisfaction among the retirees. Other personal characteristics, in contrast, including whether one was female or male or married or not, showed no clear relation to satisfaction of academics either prior to or in retirement, nor did nonprofessional activities such as volunteer work or leisure activities.

Another way that the retired academics expressed continuity in later life was that most decided to continue to live in their preretirement communities and not to begin a retirement lifestyle elsewhere. Most of the retirees, like retirees everywhere, opted to remain in the surroundings that they had known for years. The reasons they gave for staying in place conveyed a sense of ease with those familiar surroundings: this was where their home was, where their friends and perhaps their families were, where there was a community of scholars, where they could continue to enjoy the cultural and professional opportunities of their college or university community. For most, there was simply no compelling reason or even desire to leave their college or university community after retiring. True, attractions like a better climate, new professional opportunities, or a desire to be closer to children and grandchildren drew some retirees away, but they were a minority. One notable pattern that was adopted by a substantial minority of retired academics was to leave their preretirement community for several months each year, usually either to live in a better climate during the winter months or to travel extensively. In this way, people were able to maintain their established ties and associations with their preretirement communities and yet be free to try new places and new people. The academics saw this kind of flexibility as one of the bonuses of their retirement.

Activity

"I think everybody that retires must have something to do to keep them busy. I can think of nothing worse than having nothing to do. There isn't nearly enough time in my retirement. I would say they must have had something. I'm not sure it's a hobby. It must be some goal; something that will make life worth living for them when they do retire." Most of the retirees followed the advice to stay busy offered by this seventy-eight-year-old female liberal arts college musician. A commonly heard refrain from the retired academics was that they were even busier than they had been before retirement; however, for the majority of the retirees, the mix of those activities had changed considerably. In addition to the professional activities that most of them were still engaged in, there were a host of leisure and voluntary activities in which they were involved. The majority of academics said they had taken up at least one new activity in retirement, indicating some substitution of new activities for the lost work role. Those who had decided to completely substitute leisure and voluntary activities for professional work gave a number of interrelated reasons: they had worked long enough, work had become tiring or less interesting than it used to be, it was difficult to find support for their work, it was time to turn over work to younger people. All of these comments showed a willingness, even a desire, to accept a qualitative change in their lives. Professional work had clearly become of less interest to those academics, and to some it had even become aversive.

At least half of the retirees said they were involved in unpaid volunteer work at some time during their retirement; moreover, many of those voluntary activities utilized the professional skills they had built up over a lifetime. Now the academics were simply applying their professional skills in different contexts than they had prior to retirement, ranging from work with children to work in nursing homes, from involvement in national environmental concerns to local civic and cultural activities. The leisure activities in which they were engaged also reflected a very high level of activity; most were not passive pursuits. The retirees traveled, they gardened, they golfed, they sailed, they participated in arts and crafts, they took up music and writing, as well as numerous other activities. One particularly interesting aspect of their leisure activity was that so many (about one-half of the retirees), accustomed as they were to the life of the mind, took up studies outside their own professional field after retiring. What they wanted was to continue learning, to remain intellectually involved, whether it be through formal or informal channels, and the range of their intellectual endeavors was impressive — languages, art, history, archaeology, and astronomy, to name but a few.

All told, the lives of these academic retirees illustrate two important theoretical perspectives in social gerontology — activity theory and continuity theory. The former suggests that activity of one sort or another is related to positive adjustment in later life, whereas the latter suggests that continuity of as many life patterns as possible is adaptive for most people as they age.

Comparisons

We have seen the common threads, the themes, that pervaded the retirement experience of the academics. The differences in the way they experienced their retirement, however, were equally interesting and were most evident in the type of institution they came from and in terms of discipline, gender, age, and, not least, nation. Let us turn first to a major interest of this study — the variations that emerged for retirees from different types of institutions.

Institutional Comparisons

The most important way that retired academics from the various types of institutions differed in retirement was in their professional activities and commitments. Those professional involvements differed in both kind and quantity. Reflecting both the emphases of their particular institutions and their own professional commitments, liberal arts college retirees were the most likely to have continued teaching activities after formally retiring. Furthermore, such involvement in teaching was associated with their satisfaction during the retirement years. American research university and British old civic university retirees, on the other hand, were more likely to have continued publishing articles and going to professional meetings after retiring than were either their liberal arts college or comprehensive university counterparts. Retirees from the research and old civic universities were also more likely to talk about missing their work and to say that they liked having time to spend on professional activities in retirement than were the other retirees, thus highlighting the continued salience of the professional role in the lives of academics from those institutions.

What seems to emerge from these differences in professional activity and orientation among retirees from different types of institutions is that the institutional context in which they worked appeared to influence their lives not only during their preretirement careers, but also during the retirement years. Although a large majority of academics across institutions continued some sort of professional activity in retirement, it appears that any general model of retirement behavior for academics will most probably have to give significant attention to retirees from different categories of institutions.

Interestingly, there were also institutional differences in the ways the academics approached planning for retirement. The majority of academics across institutions did do some planning for retirement; however, in one key aspect — financial planning — the American liberal arts college academics did significantly less planning than did their American university counterparts. What is more, liberal arts college faculty were also less likely to have checked on retirement benefits with their college than were their university counterparts. This appears rather puzzling at first, because liberal arts college professors earned substantially lower incomes during their preretirement careers and subsequently had lower retirement incomes than did university professors. One possibility is that liberal arts college academics engaged in less financial planning for retirement because of the comparatively smaller size and complexity of their institutions and their communities. The smaller size may have exerted less pressure toward financial planning than was experienced by academics who lived in larger and more complex settings. It may also have been the case that the cost of living was lower for liberal arts college faculty, who lived in predominantly nonurban settings.

Cross-national Comparisons

Although both British and American academics were generally quite positive about retirement and engaged in high levels of professional activity in retirement, there were some notable differences between retired academics from the British old civic universities and retired academics from the American research university to whom they were compared. For one thing, although both British and American academics were likely to have continued research activity in retirement, they showed some differences in the kinds of scholarly productivity they were engaged in. British academics were more likely to publish books and chapters in retirement than were their American counterparts, as had also been the case during their preretirement careers. Yet British academics were just as likely to continue publishing articles as were American academics. Academics from the two nations also differed in a teaching-related function — external examining — which existed in the United Kingdom only. About one-tenth of the British retirees said they were engaged in such external examining, in which they read and evaluated student examinations, theses, and dissertations from other institutions in the United Kingdom and other countries, in particular the British Commonwealth nations. This was one way that a number of British academics could continue their professional activities in retirement.

Cultural and probably economic differences reflecting the greater presence of the welfare state in the United Kingdom were apparent in several aspects of the retirement process and experience of British academics. For example, fewer British academics engaged in financial planning for retirement than did American academics, and British academics also made financial plans on the average about ten years later than did their American counterparts. Furthermore, British academics were less likely to express financial concerns about retirement. These reactions and behaviors suggest that there was generally less preoccupation with economic matters among the British academics, probably reflecting the relatively greater economic safety net in the United Kingdom than in the United States.

One disadvantage of the economic situation for academic retirees in the United Kingdom, however, was that their institutions appeared less able to offer financial support for continued professional activity in retirement than did American institutions. Far fewer British retirees had office space, secretarial assistance, or laboratories available after retirement than did their American university counterparts.

This may have been why relatively fewer of the British retirees said they had checked on what university and departmental facilities were available for retired academic staff; many already knew that such facilities were limited or unavailable. Many of the British academics commented sadly on their loss of facilities and services, most frequently the loss of secretarial assistance. Some of the older men, in particular, could not type and found typing a manuscript or even writing a simple professional letter a burdensome chore. Not surprisingly, five times as many British as American academics mentioned loss of facilities and services as a negative aspect of retirement (24 percent versus 5 percent, respectively); in fact, next to loss of contact with students and colleagues, this was the negative aspect of retirement most frequently identified by British academics.

British and American academics also differed in other aspects of retirement. Whereas a large majority (about three-fourths) of the American research university retirees to whom they were compared continued to live in their preretirement community, almost one-half of the British university retirees migrated from their preretirement communities after retiring. This may have been due to the British universities being located in large urban centers, with desirable seaside and Lake District retirement communities located nearby. Because of the relatively small scale of the British Isles, retirees could migrate to these communities and still not be geographically far from relatives and preretirement friends. None of the American institutions, in contrast, were located in very large urban centers, as were both the Universities of Liverpool and Manchester; most were located in either small college or university towns or small cities, which may have been attractive to retirees.

There were also some British-American differences in how leisure time was spent in retirement. More British academics became involved in leisure activities such as hobbies, work around the house or garden, travel, and studies outside their own professional field after retiring than did their American counterparts. Gardening was particularly popular among the British retirees, probably reflecting the importance of gardening in English culture. One possible explanation for the relatively greater involvement in leisure activities among British academics after retiring may be a greater acceptance of leisure in the United Kingdom than in the United States. Alternatively, some of the leisure activities that the retired academics engaged in, such as gardening, may be more culturally normative or easily accessible (e.g., travel to the Continent) in the United Kingdom than they are in the United States.

Disciplinary Subsets

Retired academics remained professionally active across disciplines; however, the comments made by scientists suggested that it may have been more difficult for them to keep going professionally than it was for retirees from other disciplines. There were a number of reasons for this identified by the scientists themselves: they were dependent on outside money to run laboratories, and it became increasingly difficult with age to retain the extramural grant support that would pay for running those laboratories and for equipment, research assistants, and supplies; scarce laboratory space was needed for new, younger faculty; knowledge was usually very rapidly changing in their field of specialization, and it was becoming more difficult to keep up. What some of the scientists did was to shift from being a bench scientist to other related endeavors, such as consulting, writing up the research they had done in recent years, or writing textbooks or histories of their fields.

Physicians and other helping professionals, including some who had also been scientists, were often able to keep going professionally by emphasizing clinical work or patient care or by doing consulting work. To illustrate, we saw the university pediatrician who was involved in a statewide genetic consultation service or the orthopedist who consulted at a Department of Veterans' Affairs Medical Center.

Retirees from the humanities and the arts were most often able to continue their work at home or with access to college or university libraries, which they all had available. Consequently, few retirees in those disciplines complained of not having the resources to continue their work during the retirement years, and most appeared to be able to continue their scholarly or artistic activity with relative ease, at least when compared to scientists. Many retirees in the humanities in particular may have also benefited from the accretion of verbal knowledge in their fields over time, a phenomenon which psychologists refer to as "crystallized intelligence." This kind of mastery is characteristic of occupations that involve a high level of verbal skills and tends to increase with age and experience.

Gender and Age

The sex distribution of the retirees was typical of academics who came of age before the civil rights era of the 1960s and the later trend toward affirmative action in higher education in the United States. Across institutions, the vast majority of retired academics were men; even in the American liberal arts colleges, where women were the most highly represented, only one-third of the retirees were women. In the universities, in both the United States and the United Kingdom, women represented only between 17 and 19 percent of the total number of retirees.

The academic women differed from their male counterparts more in socio-demographic characteristics than in their professional and nonprofessional activities and pursuits. Like their male colleagues, the majority of female retirees remained engaged professionally: they continued to teach, to do research, to go to meetings, to keep up with their fields. Such continued professional role performance is not surprising given the societal biases that these professional women had to overcome when they undertook their careers; these were a rather select group of high-achieving women who, despite social norms prevailing at the time, had successfully navigated a nontraditional career path earlier in their lives and had continued that path into later life.

Academic women differed most from their male peers in some of the objective circumstances of their personal lives. Most notably, far fewer women than men were currently or had ever been married; only 22 percent of the women were currently married, whereas nearly all of the men (86 percent) were currently married. We cannot attribute this marital difference primarily to the greater likelihood of widowhood for women, because two-thirds of the unmarried women had never been married. In addition to the marital difference, the women's financial circumstances differed considerably from the men's. Retired women had considerably lower incomes, both pre- and postretirement, than did their male peers, with their annual retirement income averaging about one-half that of the males. Yet the women retirees did not complain about their financial situation more than did male retirees; in fact, most, like their male counterparts, said that their postretirement standard of living was about the same as preretirement, and women did not disproportionately identify financial concerns as a problematic aspect of their retirement. There are a number of possible explanations for the women's lack of dissatisfaction with their financial situation. One is that the women came to accept their lower level of compensation due to the normative gender expectations about income that prevailed at the time they came of age. Another possibility is that the women's incomes compared favorably to other occupations that were open to them at the time, such as schoolteaching or nursing. Finally, few of the women had other family members whom they needed to help support financially; most had only themselves to look after. Most of the men, in contrast, had wives, grown children, and grandchildren to consider in evaluating their entire financial picture.

What these differences mean is that many of the academic women probably had a somewhat different personal experience of retirement than did the majority of academic men. For one thing, because of the absence of a spouse and grown children, dependence on friends and siblings for support and social interaction could be expected to be greater for many of the retired women. Living arrangements likewise differed for many of the women and the men; generally, the retired men were living with their wives, whereas many of the retired women were living either with friends or alone. I interviewed more women in group retirement-type living arrangements than men; such retirement housing and retirement communities are generally populated with far more women than men. The prospect for long-term care is also different for these academic women and men, because of the greater likelihood of the women's not having immediate nuclear family members available to provide such care.

With respect to age differences among the retirees, it was clear from the interviews that increasing age, because it is associated with one or more infirmities, affected the ability to perform all kinds of activities in retirement. It was clear that the older, sicker retirees were far more limited in both their professional and nonprofessional activities than were younger retirees in good health. However, it was also clear that some retirees in their late eighties and early nineties, if their health held up reasonably well, were still active; a number of them proudly referred to the kinds of professional work they were still engaged in. Thus, it was not age per se but the complication of poor health that interfered with the preferred retirement activities of the academics. The continued involvement in some level of professional activity of the healthy very old retirees remained a touching testimonial to their lifelong commitment to an area of intellectual interest or creative endeavor.

Implications for Faculty Development and the Utilization of Older Faculty

As demographic trends in industrial nations continue to shift toward increasingly older populations, a major challenge becomes how to keep older people productive and contributing members of their society. Particularly for those older people in their sixties and early seventies, whom we call the "young-old" and who often enjoy good health, there is an abundance of free time after retirement that can be utilized in meaningful and creative ways. Many people now live one, two, or even three decades after retirement. We owe it to both those older people and their societies to continue to utilize their talents in productive ways.

Interview after interview with these retired academics showed how vitally involved they were with their lives. The retired academics, perhaps, were among the fortunate, for all their lives they lived by their minds, and for the most part they were able to continue to do so into later life. Even though the academics, like other older people, suffered declining energy and health with advancing age, they were not handicapped by being in a physically demanding occupation that was circumscribed by age. They were advantaged in having intellectual interests and activities throughout their lives that most were able to keep alive well into the retirement years.

The fact that most academics across institutions and in both nations remained professionally active in retirement suggests that it may be worthwhile for colleges and universities to provide greater opportunities for the professional growth and development of academics in the later years of their academic careers. The majority of the retirees identified the years of middle age (approximately from age forty to age sixty) as the years in which they were able to do their best professional work. This suggests that providing more opportunities for academics to enlarge, update, or even learn entirely new professional skills in the years of middle and later maturity not only would be valuable for their own professional growth and development, but also would be beneficial for their institutions. Such opportunities for faculty development might necessitate more "time-outs" from the usual academic enterprise. The loss of older faculty for short periods, however, could be more than offset by gains in individual faculty growth, productivity, and benefits for students who would have the advantage of exposure to a revitalized older faculty.

Older academics could also be utilized in more creative ways after they retired. For example, efforts have been made at starting "emeritus colleges" at various locations throughout the United States, including Southern Illinois University and Hastings College of Law in California. Essentially, these colleges have used retired academics to teach formal or informal courses in their areas of expertise, sometimes in traditional formats and sometimes in nontraditional formats, such as short courses or tutorials, or in outreach to the community. Retired academics could also be utilized to teach in off-campus programs that regular faculty are too time-constrained to participate in; this might provide retirees who wanted to continue teaching with more opportunities to do so. Such off-campus teaching by retirees might also provide a more nontraditional group of students than is found on campus with the advantage of exposure to professors with long experience in teaching, who are also probably quite heavily committed to teaching. Other possibilities for continued involvement of retired academics include being invited to give occasional guest lectures in classes in their own or other departments and being included as emeritus members of student thesis and dissertation committees. Such professional involvement can make the considerable intellectual talent and experience of retired academics available to students and also help reduce their feelings of isolation from the life of their departments and institutions.

Throughout the interviews ran the thread of the importance of institutional opportunity structures that would allow retired faculty to continue their work at some level during the retirement years. Continued opportunities for professional work in retirement, in the form of secretarial assistance, office space, laboratories, and other facilities, not only are important for continued feelings of well-being and continued integration of retirees, but also can be a way of making retirement more attractive — or at least more palatable — for older faculty who are approaching retirement age. Under the new condition of no mandatory retirement age in American higher education, it is very important for colleges and universities to develop strategies that will deal fairly and humanely with tenured faculty members at older ages. Beyond offering retirement incentives like early and phased retirement packages, making the actual experience of retirement more attractive by offering adequate information about retirement and a facilitative institutional opportunity structure to continue work may encourage the retirement of older faculty and help free some positions for the addition of younger faculty. The interviews showed that most of the academics felt that there was a need for new blood in their fields and that many were concerned with what they called "dead wood" in their faculties. Their comments revealed considerable concern about academic vitality and issues of intergenerational equity in colleges and universities.

The Future

This book reflects the experiences of a cross-section of older academics who entered retirement between the late 1970s and the late 1980s. I believe that although there may be some general principles of retirement behavior that hold across time for academics, there will undoubtedly be differences that arise among succeeding cohorts of retired academics because of the historical times they live in and the experiences they encounter during those periods. One question that arises, then, is to what degree will new cohorts of academics view their careers and their retirements in the same way as the academics represented here? We know that higher education in both the United States and the United Kingdom has been much affected by macroeconomic changes that have caused considerable belt-tightening, downsizing, and restructuring in colleges and universities. Along with this has come much heavier dependence on extramural sources of funding than was found even a decade ago. We also know that there have been some dramatic changes in the composition of the professoriate itself, not the least being the entrance of large numbers of women into the academic labor market in the last two decades. Many more of those women are married and have children than in previous cohorts of academic women; some are in dual-academic families. The experiences of those women throughout their careers and in retirement may provide some interesting variations in the general academic retirement picture.

Other major issues influencing the academic retirement experience include policy-level changes, particularly the elimination of mandatory retirement in American higher education in 1994. What will be the short- and long-term effects of the uncapping of the mandatory retirement age? Will many academics stay on until quite advanced ages, or will the uncapping affect primarily major research institutions, as the National Research Council suggests? If so, how will those research institutions cope with increasingly aged faculties and what mechanisms will they employ to try to reduce the numbers of very old faculty members? Are we headed toward an era of performance assessment of very old professors, a rather distasteful task at best for colleagues to have to deal with in the final stages of a faculty member's career? Or a reevaluation of our current conceptions of tenure? In an effort to encourage older academics to retire and thereby provide opportunities for young academics, will colleges and universities offer yet more retirement incentive packages? And how will these packages and perhaps the option of phased retirement affect the retirement experience of future retirees? All of these issues are serious ones that may have an impact on the careers and lives of future generations of academic retirees.

Although this book is the first to include cross-national case materials on retired academics, it does not include the experiences of non-Western and non-English-speaking retirees. It would be interesting to know how the experiences of such academics compare to those of the academics represented here. We have seen that there were some differences in the lives and experiences of retired academics from two Western, English-speaking nations. It is likely that there are even more marked differences among academics who live in more disparate social, cultural, and economic contexts.

A Concluding Note

Attempting to accurately portray the retirement experiences shared in over four hundred interviews with retired and retiring academics is a daunting and humbling task. These retired academic men and women speak for themselves; I have merely tried to integrate and interpret what their own voices so eloquently expressed. From them I learned much, not only about their retirements, but about the full span of their lives and their careers. Most of the academics were quite open and willing to share their thoughts with me; others were more reticent. The most touching were the very old, the ones who recollected events from an often dim past; those were the retirees who often asked me to come back to visit. In my mind's eye, I see pictures of them all: of many who showed me the evidence of their life's work — their books, their articles, their paintings, their slides; of those who spoke with enormous affection of the students they had produced; of those who felt still part of their college or university and those who felt utterly forgotten; of elderly husbands and wives caring for each other; of nursing home residents surrounded by books, still attempting to be professional despite infirmity. They were a remarkable, highly talented, and articulate group of people and remained so in old age. I learned much not only about their disciplines and their careers, but about their lives. I thank them for allowing me a window into those lives.

Appendix A Sources

General

The only two previous books that included qualitative case materials from retired professors were studies of the experiences of TIAA-CREF annuitants by Mark H. Ingraham (in collaboration with James M. Mulanaphy), *My Purpose Holds: Reactions and Experiences in Retirement of TIAA-CREF Annuitants* (New York: Teachers Insurance and Annuity Association/College Retirement Equities Fund, 1974), and a follow-up ten years later by Mario A. Milletti, *Voices of Experience: 1500 Retired People Talk about Retirement* (New York: Teachers Insurance and Annuity Association/College Retirement Equities Fund, 1984). Although these works are invaluable resources, they include all TIAA-CREF annuitants and are therefore not restricted to retired professors. Furthermore, they are based on mailed questionnaires rather than on extensive personal interviews.

Other general resources include the National Center on Educational Statistics, *Digest of Educational Statistics* (Washington, D.C.: United States Government Printing Office, 1994), and the National Research Council, *Ending Mandatory Retirement for Tenured Faculty* (Washington, D.C.: National Academy Press, 1991). William C. Lane, "Recent Trends in Faculty Retirement Research," in a paper presented at the March 1994 annual meeting of the Midwest Sociological Society, offers an overview of research on academic retirement since the 1950s.

Getting Ready: Preparation for Retirement

Interest in this topic was seen as early as the 1950s, with a study at New York University by Margaret M. Benz, "A Study of Faculty and Administrative Staff Who Retired from NYU," *Journal of Educational Sociology* 31 (1958): 282–293. A number of studies are useful in showing that retired professors urge professors who are approaching retirement to plan ahead: to discuss retirement with relatives and friends; to investigate what perquisites will be available from their institution after they retire; and to plan for finances, activities, use of time, and where to live. See Benz, "Faculty and Administrative Staff"; Leonard Gernant, "What 814 Retired Professors Say about Retirement," *Gerontologist* 12 (1980): 349–353; Ingraham, *My Purpose Holds*; Eugene A. Friedmann and William C. Lane, "Academics and the Changing Nature of Retirement," *Educational Considerations* 8 (1980): 10–14; and Elon H. Moore, "Professors in Retirement," *Journal of Gerontology* 6 (1951): 243–252. The most recent survey of the retirement plans of TIAA-CREF annuitants is by Kevin Gray, *Retirement Plans and Expectations of TIAA-CREF Policyholders* (New York: Teachers Insurance and Annuity Association/College Retirement Equities Fund, 1989). It should be pointed out, however, that fewer than half of the respondents in that TIAA-CREF survey were professors.

For the relationship between planning for retirement and work after retirement, see Gerda Fillenbaum and George Maddox, "Work after Retirement: An Investigation into Some Psychologically Relevant Variables," *Gerontologist* 14 (1974): 418–424. Retirement preparation among special incentive early retirees is examined in Diane Kell and Carl V. Patton, "Reaction to Induced Early Retirement," *Gerontologist* 18 (1978): 173–179. Comparative information on the retirement planning process of professors from different kinds of institutions can be found in Lorraine T. Dorfman, Karen A. Conner, William Ward, and Jean B. Tompkins, "Reactions of Professors to Retirement: A Comparison of Retired Faculty from Three Types of Institutions," *Research in Higher Education* 20 (1984): 89–102. For a cross-national comparison of retirement planning among academics, see Lorraine T. Dorfman, "British and American Academics in Retirement," *Educational Gerontology* 15 (1989): 25–40.

Where to Live: Staying in or Leaving the Preretirement Community

Few studies of retired professors have examined where they live after retiring, even though choice of housing and retirement migration are major decisions that greatly affect quality of life in retirement. The housing and migration plans of TIAA-CREF annuitants are discussed in Gray, *Retirement Plans and Expectations*. Housing and migration choices of TIAA-CREF annuitants who have already retired, as well as the reasons for those residential choices, are described by Ingraham, *My Purpose Holds*; and Milletti, *Voices of Experience*. Comparative information on professors from different kinds of institutions who stayed in or left their preretirement communities after retiring is given in Dorfman et al., "Reactions of Professors." The only cross-national comparison of professors' decision to stay in or leave their preretirement communities is found in Dorfman, "British and American Academics."

Experiencing Retirement

Most of the studies of retired academics, spanning more than four decades, indicate that they are generally positive about retirement and adjust well to retirement. Early works during the 1950s describing professors' reactions to retirement include Benz, "Faculty and Administrative Staff"; Moore, "Professors in Retirement"; and Ruth Aisenberg, "What Happens to Old Psychologists?" in Robert Kastenbaum, ed., *New Thoughts on Old Age* (New York: Springer, 1964). The 1970s are represented by a number of studies, including Robert J. Havighurst, William J. McDonald, Pamela J. Perun, and Robert B. Snow, *Social Scientists and Educators: Lives after Sixty* (Chicago: Committee on Human Development, 1976; mimeographed); Ingraham, *My Purpose Holds*; Peter J. Kratcoski, James H. Huber, and Ruth Gavlak, "Retirement Satisfaction among Emeritus Professors," *Industrial Gerontology* 1 (1974): 78–81; and Alan R. Rowe's series of studies on retired scientists: "The Retirement of Academic Scientists," *Journal of Gerontology* 27 (1972): 113–118, "Scientists in Retirement," *Journal of Gerontology* 28 (1973): 345–350, and "Retired Academics and Research Activity," *Journal of Gerontology* 31 (1976): 456–461. A few studies undertaken during the 1970s focused on reactions to retirement among special incentive early retirees; see Kell and Patton, "Induced Early Retirement"; and Carl V. Patton, "Early Retirement in Academia: Making the Decision," *Gerontologist* 17 (1977): 347–353. Studies in the 1980s include Karen B. Conner, Lorraine T. Dorfman, and Jean B. Tompkins, "Life Satisfaction of Retired Professors: The Contribution of Work, Health, Income, and Length of Retirement," *Educational Gerontology* 11 (1985): 337–347; Lenard W. Kaye and Abraham Monk, "Sex Role Traditions and Retirement from Academe," *Gerontologist* 24 (1984): 420–426; Dorfman et al., "Reactions of Professors"; Dorfman, "British and American Academics"; and Milletti, *Voices of Experience*. The 1990s are represented by few studies: Lorraine T. Dorfman, "Academics and the Transition to Retirement," *Educational Gerontology* 18 (1992): 343–363; and Thomas Walz, John Craft, and Nancee Blum, "Social Work Faculty in Retirement: A National Study," *Journal of Social Work Education* 27 (1991): 60–72. Several sources describing professors' evaluation of retirement are worthy of note because they examine the relationship between such factors as health, financial status, and activity patterns and satisfaction during retirement; see Conner et al., "Life Satisfaction"; Kratcoski et al., "Retirement Satisfaction"; and Dorfman, "Transition to Retirement."

Activities in Retirement

Activity patterns of retired professors are arguably the most researched area of academic retirement. Theoretical explanations for activity in retirement such as continuity and disengagement are addressed in works by Robert C. Atchley, "Disengagement among Professors," *Journal of Gerontology* 26 (1971): 476–480; Lorraine T. Dorfman, "Emeritus Professors: Correlates of Professional Activity in Retirement," *Research in Higher Education* 12 (1980): 301–316; Lorraine T. Dorfman, "Emeritus Professors: Correlates of Professional Activity in Retirement II," *Research in Higher Education* 14 (1981): 147–160; Dorfman, "British and American Academics"; Dorfman, "Transition to Retirement"; Friedmann and Lane, "Academics and the Changing Nature of Retirement"; and Paul Roman and Philip Taietz, "Organizational Structure and Disengagement," *Gerontologist* 7 (1967): 147–152. For discussions of level of participation in professional roles and activities during retirement, see Benz, "Faculty and Administrative Staff"; Conner et al., "Life Satisfaction"; Lorraine T. Dorfman, Karen A. Conner, Jean B. Tompkins, and William Ward, "Retired Professors and Professional Activity: A Comparative Study of Three Types of Institutions," *Research in Higher Education* 17 (1982): 249–266; Dorfman, "Emeritus Professors II" and "British and American Academics"; Fillenbaum and Maddox, "Work after Retirement"; Robert J. Havighurst, William F. McDonald, Leo Mauelen, and Joseph Mazel, "Male Social Scientists: Lives after Sixty," *Gerontologist* 19 (1979): 55–60; Havighurst et al., *Social Scientists and Educators*; Ingraham, *My Purpose Holds*; Kaye and Monk, "Sex Role Traditions"; Kratcoski et al., "Retirement Satisfaction"; Milletti, *Voices of Experience*; Moore, "Professors in Retirement"; Roman and Taietz, "Organizational Structure"; and Rowe, "Academic Scientists," "Scientists in Retirement," "Research Activity," and his short report, "Retirement of Emeritus Professors of the University of Chicago and the University of Wisconsin," *Psychological Reports* 59 (1986): 721–722. Arnold Auerbach, in "Emeritus Professors: Engagement and Involvement," *Educational Gerontology* 10 (1984): 277–287, shows how the professional skills of retired academics can be utilized in such ways as an emeritus college. Robert B. Snow and Robert J. Havighurst develop an interesting typology of "maintainers" of professional activity versus "transformers," who adopt a nonprofessional activity pattern in retirement; see "Lifestyle Types and Patterns of Retirement of Educators," *Gerontologist* 17 (1977): 545–552. This study, however, was limited to college and university presidents and other high-ranking administrators in higher education.

For a discussion of "local" and "cosmopolitan" professional orientations and level of professional activity among retired academics, see Dorfman, "Emeritus Professors," "Emeritus Professors II," and "British and American Academics"; and two papers by William C. Lane, "Faculty Retirement: Locals, Cosmopolitans, and Professional Commitment" (32nd Annual Scientific Meeting of the Gerontological Society of America, Washington, D.C., November 1979), and "Locals and Cosmopolitans: Patterns of Professional Activity among Retired Faculty" (Eastern Sociological Society Meeting, Philadelphia, Penn., March 1982). Fillenbaum and Maddox, "Work after Retirement," provide an excellent analysis of factors related to working for pay after retirement. Differences in working for pay by discipline are addressed by Neil C. Bull and Dianne Powell, "The Impact of Retirement on University Faculty" (paper presented at the Midwest Sociological Society Annual Meeting, Des Moines, Ia., April 1982). A few studies address the relationship between continued professional activity in retirement and retirement satisfaction; see Conner et al., "Life Satisfaction"; Dorfman, "Transition to Retirement"; Kratcoski et al., "Retirement Satisfaction"; and Snow and Havighurst, "Lifestyle Types." Few studies examine sex differences in activities of retired academics; see Havighurst et al., *Social Scientists and Educators*; Kaye and Monk, "Sex Role Traditions"; and Walz et al., "Social Work Faculty." The only cross-national comparison of professional activities of retired academics is found in Dorfman, "British and American Academics."

Professors also participate in a wide variety of leisure, service, and other nonprofessional activities in retirement, many of them resembling those of other retirement groups. Good descriptions of these activities can be found in Benz, "Faculty and Administrative Staff"; Dorfman, "British and American Academics"; Ingraham, *My Purpose Holds*; Kratcoski et al., "Retirement Satisfaction"; and Milletti, *Voices of Experience*.

Appendix B Interview Schedules

U.S. Research University and U.K. Old Civic University Interview

Introduction: We believe that people about to retire might better anticipate the problems and satisfactions of retirement if they could learn from
persons who are already retired. We would appreciate your advice to
present and future retirees based on your experiences.

(Reactions to retirement)

A1. As far as you are concerned, what are the *best* things about
retirement?

A2. What are the *worst* things about retirement?

A3. What are some suggestions you would make for those who are soon
to retire?

(The professional role)

A4. People often identify such things as contact with colleagues and
students, the rewards of research and teaching, etc., as important to
them in their professional role. Are there things you *miss* about
your professional activities before retirement?
Yes _____ No _____ If YES, *what* do you miss?

A5. What do you consider to be your special strengths professionally
during the course of your career prior to retirement?

A6. Do you see yourself as continuing some of the professional
activities that you were involved in prior to retirement?
Yes _____ No _____ If YES, please tell me about them.

A7. What kinds of things do you need to do to keep current in your
field?

(New activities in retirement)

A8. Please tell me about any leisure, service or other activities you have
become involved in mainly *since* your retirement.

(Role of the University)

A9. What information or advice from the University administrative staff did you receive about retirement before you retired from the University?

A10. How can the University best help faculty in the transition to retirement?

A11. Do you think it is better for a person to retire all at once, or more gradually, by reducing the number of hours worked?

A12. (U.S.) Would you have continued to work beyond age 68 if retirement were not mandatory at the University at that age?
(U.K.) Would you have liked to continue work beyond the age you retired?

Yes _____ No _____ Why or why not?

A13. Do you feel that mandatory retirement at the University should be eliminated?

Yes _____ No _____ Why or why not?

(Reasons for remaining in the local community)

A14. (U.S.) At the time of your retirement, did you consider leaving Iowa City?
(U.K.) Did you continue to live in your preretirement community after you retired?

Yes _____ No _____ Why or why not?

A15. That is all the questions I have. Are there any things you might like to add that we have not talked about?

Liberal Arts College and Comprehensive University Interview

Introduction: We believe that people about to retire might better anticipate the problems and satisfactions of retirement if they could learn from persons who are already retired. We would appreciate your advice to present and future retirees based on your experiences.

(Reactions to retirement)

A1. As far as you are concerned, what are the *best* things about retirement?

A2. What are the *worst* things about retirement?

A3. What are some suggestions you would make for those who are soon to retire?

(The professional role)

A4. People often identify such things as contact with colleagues and students, the rewards of research and teaching, etc., as important to them in their professional role. Are there things you *miss* about your professional activities?

Yes _____ No _____ If YES, *what* do you miss?

A5. What do you consider to be your special professional strengths during your career prior to retirement?

A6. Are you continuing some of the professional activities that you were involved in prior to retirement?

Yes _____ No _____ If YES, please tell me what they are.

A7. Is it important to you to keep current in your field?

Yes _____ No _____ If YES, what kinds of things do you do to keep current?

(New activities in retirement)

A8. Please tell me about any leisure, service or other activities you have become involved in mainly *since* your retirement.

(Role of the University or College)

A9. In order of importance and usefulness to you, what were the sources of information or advice you received about retirement before you retired?

A10. What information or advice from the University (College) administrative staff did you receive about retirement before you retired?

A11. What information, services or benefits has the University (College) provided for you since your retirement?

A12. What information, services or benefits would you have liked to receive from the University (College) but did not?

A13. How can the University (College) best help faculty in the transition to retirement?

A14. Do you think it is better for a person to retire all at once, or more gradually?

All at once _____ More gradually _____

If MORE GRADUALLY, how should this be done?

A15. Would you have continued to work beyond age 68 (65) if retirement were not mandatory at the University (College) at that age?

Yes _____ No _____ Why or why not?

A16. Do you feel that mandatory retirement at the University (College) should be eliminated?

Yes _____ No _____ Why or why not?

(Preparation for retirement)

A17. How important to you in coming to your own decision to retire were the attitudes of others (such as family, friends and colleagues)?

A18. What (if any) steps did you take in preparation for retirement?

(Reasons for remaining in the local community)

A19. At the time of your retirement, did you consider leaving the local University (College) community?

Yes _____ No _____ Why or why not?

A20. That is all the questions I have. Are there any things you might like to add that we have not talked about?

Transition to Retirement Preretirement Interview

Introduction: We believe that other people who are about to retire might better anticipate the problems and satisfactions of retirement if they could learn from persons like you who are approaching retirement.

(Reactions to approaching retirement)

A1. People anticipate their retirement with many different kinds of feelings. In general, how do you feel about your approaching retirement?

A2. Right now, what do you expect to be the best things about retirement?

A3. What do you expect to be the most negative things about retirement?

A4. Sometimes people nearing retirement say that they notice changes in the behavior of their colleagues and students. Have you noticed any of these changes?

Yes _____ No _____ If YES, please tell me about them.

A5. From your own experience approaching retirement, what are some suggestions you would make for others who are soon to retire?

(The professional role)

A6. People often identify such things as contact with colleagues and students, the rewards of research and teaching, etc., as important to them in their professional role. Are there things you expect to *miss* about your professional activities before retirement?

Yes _____ No _____ If YES, what do you expect to miss?

A7. What do you consider to be your special professional strengths during the course of your career?

A8. Do you expect to continue some of the professional activities that you were involved in prior to retirement?

Yes _____ No _____ If YES, please tell me about them.

(New activities in retirement)

A9. Are there any new leisure, service or other activities you plan to become involved in after you retire, or that you expect to spend considerably more time in than at present?

(Role of the University)

A10. What information or advice have you received from the University administrative staff about retirement?

A11. In what ways do you think the University can best help faculty in the transition to retirement?

A12. Do you think it is better for a person to retire all at once, or more gradually, by reducing the number of hours worked?

(If retiring at age 70)

A13. Would you continue to work beyond the current retirement age if retirement were not mandatory at the University?

Yes _____ No _____ Why or why not?

(If retiring before age 70)

Why did you decide to retire before the mandatory age?

A14. Do you feel that mandatory retirement at the University should be eliminated?

Yes _____ No _____ Why or why not?

(Reasons for leaving or remaining in Iowa City)

A15. Are you planning to continue to live in Iowa City when you retire?

Yes _____ No _____ Why or why not?

If YES, do you expect to live here year round?

Yes _____ No _____

A16. That is all the questions I have for this part of the interview. Are there any things you might like to add that we have not talked about?

Transition to Retirement Postretirement Interview

Introduction: We believe that other people who are about to retire or who have recently retired might better anticipate both the satisfactions and problems of retirement if they could learn from people like you who have recently retired. I would appreciate your comments based on the experiences you have had so far in retirement.

(Reactions to retirement)

A1. All things considered, how have you found the first year of retirement to be?

A2. What are the things you like best about retirement so far?

A3. What are the things you like least about retirement?

A4. What (if any) surprises have you found about being retired?

A5. From your own experiences in the past year, what suggestions would you make for others who are soon to retire?

(The professional role)

A6. People often identify such things as contact with colleagues and students, the rewards of teaching and research, etc., as important to them in their professional role. Are there things you *miss* about your professional activities before retirement?

Yes _____ No _____ If YES, *what* do you miss?

A7. Do you see yourself as continuing some of the professional activities that you were involved in prior to retirement?

Yes _____ No _____ If YES, please tell me about them.

(New activities in retirement)

A8. Please tell me about any leisure, service or other activities you have become involved in mainly since your retirement.

(Role of the University)

A9. Now that you are retired, are there any ways that you think the University could better help faculty in the transition to retirement?

A10. Do you think it is better to retire all at once, or more gradually, by reducing the number of hours worked?

A11. Are you glad you retired when you did?

Yes _____ No _____ Why or why not?

(Migrating or not migrating after retirement)

A12. If you had to do it over, would you have stayed in (or left) Iowa City?

Yes _____ No _____ Why is that?

A13. That is all the questions I have for this part of the interview. Are there any things you might like to add that we haven't talked about?

Index